DEAR McSWEENEY'S,
I write this letter from the bath in my apartment in San Francisco. It is the seventh week of the shelter-in-place order, and if I have learned anything, it is that every room in the apartment can feel like a fresh discovery if only I put my mind to it. Basically, I take cues from my cat.

Having been an indoor cat for five years now, she's got the whole shelter-in-place bit down. I admire the way she enters and exits rooms, like she's been pushed by a gust of wind. We come into my writing room in the morning in this manner, she to meow before the highest spot on a shelf until I lift her onto it, and I to sit at my desk. She sleeps as I work on morning pages. A few hours later, when I am done, she shakes herself awake and yawns in my direction. I fetch her down and we prance to the kitchen to get a snack. Sometimes, if I have any, we share an avocado (she likes it but only if I mush it and feed it to her from my fingertip); other times, I eat an apple and pour three (or six) treats into her bowl. The next part she came up with: We each take up one of the slanted rectangles of sunlight that fall on the living room floor and sunbathe. I put on drone music for us to think to. We shift every few minutes so as to always be under our individual spotlights. Then off we go to the bath, where I read (mostly anthropology), and she, at times, balances on the tub's ledge and dips her tail in the water. We dry off and don't see each other until nighttime, when I pour catnip on the rug for her, and a glass of wine for myself. I try to write at night sometimes, which has been going great,

considering I cope with tough situations by filling my hours with work.

Once a week, I go to a cemetery. They are some of the few green places in the city that are open and uncrowded. I'd be lying if I said this is a new behavior. I have always loved cemeteries for how they provide such rare and abstract histories. So far during quarantine, I have visited a natural burial ground in Purissima, San Francisco National Cemetery, the Chinese Cemetery in Daly City, and the Presidio Pet Cemetery, along with several regular, unaffiliated cemeteries. The Pet Cemetery has been my favorite by far. It served as the burial ground for the rodents, dogs, cats, parakeets, a Mr. Iguana, and fish of the military families who lived in the Presidio when it was an army base. Most of the burials date back to the 1960s, but a few go as far back as the '50s. OUR KNUCKLE HEAD—PARAKEET TO PARADISE one grave marker (plywood, painted white) reads. LOUISE—BELOVED RAT, FRIEND reads another. My favorite: SCHMELLY WE MISS YOU, with a drawn portrait of a round-faced cat.

On my time off, I have virtual cocktail hours and have hosted two Zoom dance parties for women of color. My apartment windows face a federal court building, and once upon a time I would have worried about being seen performing such an intimate and personal ritual as dancing, by judiciary workers no less, but now I don't mind at all. It seems to me there is a kindness to being seen now—a sharing, through our gaze, of being human. I haven't seen any judiciary workers in the building, or much of anyone. One day I saw a security guard. It was the middle of the day and I was drinking tea and stretching. He paused at a stairway. I lifted my hand and waved. After a moment, he did too.

Yours in quarantine,

INGRID ROJAS CONTRERAS
SAN FRANCISCO, CA

DEAR McSWEENEY'S,

The Grove in Los Angeles is the kind of amalgamated monstrosity that might be possible only in Southern California. It's an outdoor mall made to simulate a certain kind of pedestrian experience, one you might find on the quaint Main Street of a small town circa 1954. Except it doesn't evoke only 1954 in small-town America. No, the Grove collapses time and space in the service of shopping, combining Italianate architectural flourishes with art deco details, adjacent to the old-timey, faux-rural charm of the Farmers Market. A movie theater, a Barnes & Noble, a Cheesecake Factory, and an American Girl store anchor this temporal and geographical morass.

Near the east end of the mall there's a plaza with a massive fountain and a pristine green lawn, where people gather to watch outdoor movie screenings in the summer. In December, as if to stretch the surreality of the Christmas season in Southern California to its absolute limit, the Grove's operators churn out fake snow; kids wait in line to go "sledding" and sit on Santa's lap under the fantasy-busting sun. There are tracks running down the mall's Main Street and every so often a trolley full of mildly disappointed tourists crawls

toward the plaza, moving slowly and honking frequently so as not to hit the mildly annoyed shoppers.

In short, the Grove is an absurd place. It's also where I spent much of my time as a high school student.

High school Ismail was not a cool kid. He did not hang out in galleries in West Hollywood or street fashion stores on Fairfax. He didn't skate on the Venice Beach boardwalk. His comfort zones were strip malls in Koreatown, 7-Eleven parking lots in Mid-City, and local parks. He lived in Baldwin Hills, in South Los Angeles, but many of his friends lived in West Hollywood, Koreatown, Santa Monica, and other neighborhoods far from his.

Hanging at the Grove was an accommodation to geography: the sprawl of the city was unkind to my friends and me, carless adolescents that we were, and even if the mall wasn't equidistant from all of our homes, it *was* easily accessible. I could take a single bus north up La Brea and then walk down sparse Third Street with its inward-facing condominium complexes. I'd pass Pan Pacific Park, where kids took it upon themselves to divide the lawn on the park's southern end into soccer fields during the weekends. I was terrible at soccer but I'd join the Latinx and Korean kids for a game sometimes.

Looking back on those soccer games, I can see how unusual they were. Los Angeles is a segregated city, after all—both race- and class-wise—but that division is hard to see in places like the Grove and the surrounding neighborhoods. Malls and certain other commercial spaces are the city's lights in the night: no matter their race,

Angelenos flitter to them like moths. The Grove and its cousins—Beverly Center, Westfield Century City, the Fox Hills Mall, to name a few—draw multiracial and class-diverse crowds who all want to shop at Levi's, Nike, and the Apple Store. In that sense malls are the city's pristine spaces, free from both its history of racial segregation and the specter of encroaching gentrification. People drive to them so they can participate in a simulation of urban heterogeneity, then they return to the histories that find material expression in their segregated neighborhoods. One can think of the Grove's vague temporal and spatial dimensions as a part of that historical erasure.

Though of course that's not what I was thinking then as I walked with my friends through its ersatz village. The Grove filled me with wonder, if I'm being honest. In my version of Los Angeles, the repercussions of the 1992 Rodney King Rebellion—which took place largely in poor southern Los Angeles neighborhoods—were still evident for all to see. Some buildings that were charred in that year's violence remained so, black soot coating their paint. Driving down Florence Avenue, you could see the abandoned storefronts and empty lots that signaled capital's flight from the region. Adequate public space was sparse; the blocks were so long and the tree coverage so meager that on hot days walking around ranged from profoundly unpleasant to outright impossible. History was unbearably present in South Los Angeles.

By contrast, the Grove was so glossy, so spacious, so new. I loved the Italianate storefronts, the lawn, the fountain, and, yes, even the trolley—it was all fairly exciting. I think that was why, in my mind, the Grove became a representation of all that South Los Angeles was not, the opposite of the symbolic lack that people saw when they looked at my home. Sitting on the doorstep of wealthy West Los Angeles, a stone's throw from the moneyed gleam of Beverly Hills' storefronts and auto dealers, it was an escape from history. The Grove and its environs were spared 1992's violence, which the LAPD kept contained largely in black and Hispanic areas.

What I said earlier about why my friends and I hung out at the Grove wasn't completely accurate. The truth behind my northward sojourns was that few of my friends really wanted to visit my part of the city, no matter how middle-class my particular neighborhood was. Many of them lived above the 10, the freeway that slashes its way across the center of the city and acts as an unofficial border. Its logic is elegant, brutal: you've got your relatively wealthy neighborhoods, like Mid-City and Fairfax, to the north of the freeway, and your poorer neighborhoods, like Crenshaw and Exposition Park, to the south. Of course, there is also poverty to the north and wealth to the south, but that reality hardly matters. The freeway is just a convenient shorthand for marking who should be where, for who deserves what, for what is possible in one place and what must remain impossible in another.

So imagine my surprise when I sat down in early June 2020 to watch a livestream of Black Lives Matter protests in Los Angeles, and saw that, of all the streets demonstrators could have been marching down, they had convened on Third Street. A suspiciously old LAPD cruiser was burning, but not anywhere near South Los Angeles—it was on Beverly Boulevard, which sits just north of the Grove. Vandals were spray-painting and bashing in windows at the Farmers Market adjacent to the mall, and trying to break into the Whole Foods across the street. Cops had assembled along Fairfax Avenue to head off the protesters, apparently afraid of what might happen if the march moved west into Beverly Hills. Over the next week, similar protests erupted in West Hollywood, near the In-N-Out Burger that my friends and I frequented, and in Santa Monica, along the promenade, where we would sit and eat frozen yogurt in the summer. These were the pristine neighborhoods, the ahistorical lights in the night, suddenly made ugly, their beauty marred.

I couldn't help but smile in satisfaction. History had finally made itself known in those absurd precincts too.

All best,

ISMAIL MUHAMMAD
OAKLAND, CA

DEAR McSWEENEY'S,
Here's a joke: A priest, a nun, and a rabbit walk into a blood bank to donate blood. The rabbit says, "I think I might be a type O." That's it; that's the funny part. In a different time, I'd be able to write more funny parts into this letter. I would rather write you at a different time, even another freaky time, but differently freaky, Rick James freaky, Halloween freaky, sideshow freaky. I would be so happy to be writing you from the eye of

some personal catastrophe instead of a global one. Not that I am in the eye of anything. I am slowly walking on the treadmill desk that I bought to help my back problems but which is now serving as a partial solution to my problem of being quarantined inside my apartment as a pandemic surges across the globe. (I guess I am in the center in some way, by being in New York City, where the vastly underreported number of cases multiplies enormously day by day.)

I've been sodden with dark thoughts, like about how this country has been at war for my whole life—so many wars—but I have never had to wait in a bread line or stay in my home or do without eggs or milk or toilet paper or wonder when our lives will return to something called normal or if, on the other side of this, we and the people we love will have our lives at all. I can't help the part of me that feels—about those of us cloistered in our homes who have not already experienced these hardships for other reasons, like poverty—that this small taste of fear and deprivation is the thinnest sliver of the suffering experienced by the people at the other end of the wars our country has fought. There's more, but I'll leave it at that.

This morning I finished editing my third book, which will be published in March 2021. It has been easy to lose myself in this close work—combing through sentences, shuffling paragraphs, deleting overused words, muttering under my breath as the hours slip by. I try not to think about the final product, because it's hard to imagine anyone having an appetite for intricately constructed literary essays about the mindfuck of adolescent girlhood right now, and I'm struggling to imagine a time beyond the present. Panic seems to sour the stomach for anything but news about the source of panic or escapist material. I have been afraid of finishing my book edits because that will mean it is time to begin writing something new. In that sense, I am glad to have this small assignment. A letter is among the easier things to write—the audience is narrowed to a single doorway, which is sometimes easier to walk through than the whole wide world and all its infinite directions.

Yesterday, my partner walked into the room and read me the Pablo Neruda poem "I Explain a Few Things," whose first half includes the lines: "do you remember my house with balconies where / June light smothered flowers in your mouth? / Brother, brother! / Everything / was great shouting, salty goods, / heaps of throbbing bread." Being inside of that poem as she read it felt almost too lush—the lilacs and poppies, the "lean face of Spain / like an ocean of leather," the "dogs and children," and especially the heaps of throbbing bread. I felt a kind of voluptuous scream roil in me—mournful and hungry—then settle. The second half of the poem turns dark: "And one morning all was aflame / and one morning the fires / came out of the earth / devouring people / and from then on fire... / Come and see the blood in the streets!" At these lines, I felt something else ignite in my chest, the anger that had stopped me from reading the newspaper the last two days. My eyes burned, but I didn't (couldn't?) cry.

A week ago—so much has changed, it feels like months—I went for a walk around the park with my friend Syreeta, minding the distance between our two bodies and from those of the few people we passed. We talked about feeling futile at our desks, how hard it is to imagine the readers who will eventually face the words we are typing right now. Syreeta is writing to remember the overlooked history and stories of black Americans in a region no one ever connects to them: the American heartland. As we moved single file, maintaining six feet between us to make way for another walker, she shouted over her shoulder, "You want to know the word that came into my mind the other day when I was thinking about the book?" I nodded. "*Elegy,*" she said.

"I am going to tell you all that is happening to me," Neruda writes at the beginning of his poem, which is about the longing for a time that has passed and the fury at leaders who do not lead, who allow war to ravage a country and its people, who exile Neruda's beautiful Spanish street to the past. I think a lot these days about how the things that are happening to us are so often not what is happening *around* us. Around us are the familiar walls, the humming machine, the glowing screens, day after day. Inside us is a kaleidoscope of feeling: the horror whirls, unspooled by our imaginations as we read the headlines ("the blood in the streets"), the hunger for heaps of throbbing bread and the clatter of crowded restaurants, this longing for bodies that also remember what we remember.

My friend and I stood at the end of her block to finish our conversation, unsure if we would be allowed to walk tomorrow. When we said goodbye, we wrapped our arms around our own bodies, pretending to hold each other.

Love,

MELISSA FEBOS
NEW YORK, NY

DEAR McSWEENEY'S,

I live in Los Angeles, as you know, and though I don't consider myself a Los Angelean (I was born in Ventura), I have resided in LA County for twenty-eight years and am employed there as a comedian of stand-up. One of the cultural aspects of Southern California that I have embraced is the commitment to communicating one's minute shifts in emotion in real time. And so, this letter.

This letter is to inform you that, although I will continue to subscribe to *McSweeney's*, I will no longer consider myself a Subscriber, per se. Yes, I will continue to read your magazine, and I would like it to be mailed to the same address, but I want to be clear: my relationship with you has changed. I don't want you to take it personally (as I don't take Who You Are personally), but I also need you to know that there is now a considerable boundary between us, despite the external architecture of our correspondence remaining the same.

I'm trying to be more authentic in every area of my life. I have some lifelong friendships that have long brought up uncomfortable feelings for me. Like the occasional irritation with my pal Krishna, who has two margaritas and then hugs me too hard, or the boredom that comes over me when my other friend Argus doesn't have any

exciting news from therapy to tell me. Suddenly one day, during my morning plunge into my unheated plunge pool, I realized that I deserve more. I deserve more than these below-par human connections. So I let every one of my two (2) friends know that though I'll still see them, and will participate in birthday celebrations and holiday gatherings, I'm no longer a Friend with a capital *F*. I'm seeking.

Furthermore, I recently informed my manager, Bruce Smith of Omnipop Talent Group, that though I will continue using his services, I am no longer his Client. He was (predictably) defensive and borderline abusive: "Is this like when you went to clown college?" And, yes, I did take an intensive two-weekend mime workshop that meant that whenever I went anywhere, even to a stand-up gig or voiceover job, I had to maintain silence and wear a red rubber nose. A lot of people laughed at first, but when they saw my focus and grim determination, they stopped. If I've learned anything from my French Cirque du Soleil–trained teacher Claude, true comedy isn't about getting laughs. Comedy is my essential wound.

Yes, in my *off* time, I can paint intuitively, develop organic fruit-juice perfumes, and swing dance, but for up to twenty hours a week I have to go into a voiceover studio—bright offices in Burbank, California, filled with plants (planted by other gardeners) and art (painted by other painters)—or a comedy club with unlimited free food, and it's killing me. I'm going to kill myself. And when I say that, I mean it metaphorically. A "friend" once dialed 911 after I said this several times in an hour, and now I have to edit myself. But

I'm done with people-pleasing. Even if it means that an ambulance shows up.

A list of things I no longer identify as (though still hold space for):

· a 12-stepper
· a candidate, now and always, for perfect relationships and wealth
· a mensch
· a pre-mother
· a lizard owner
· a woman with a history of mental illness

Just call me Maria. And it's Ma-reeeeeeeeee-ah, not Ma-ri-a.

And if you could publish this letter anonymously, but credit my writing? Also, please acknowledge that you received this letter via a letter of your own, but address it only to "Resident" plus my address, to respect my new boundaries.

Wow. I'm having a lot of feelings come up while writing this. Residual anger that I need to release. I feel hurt by you. You, in all my years of reading your magazine—you haven't ever published my poetry. I realize that I've never asked you to do that, nor have I submitted any poems, and I take full responsibility for my part in that, but for twelve years I've been writing a memoir prose poem about a roller skating experience I had in 1985. I've got this four-CVS-notebooks-long manuscript, and you've never thought to ask, *Hey, are you writing anything epic?* I know we're not at that place anymore in our relationship, and I say this just so you know that your actions (or lack of them) affect other people. I can't stay silent anymore.

Okay! Whew! :)!!!!! I love where we are at now. I am no longer a Subscriber; you're no longer *McSweeney's*, and we're in this new place of not knowing.

I don't mean to sound ungrateful—gratitude is so important. I am grateful for my late-model RAV4, a million-dollar home paid off, and a little over a million in retirement at the age of forty-nine, but those things are just Band-Aids on a violent ax-slash through my still-beating heart. People talk about warfare, but I'm bleeding out every day over a laptop with a view of the San Bernardino mountains. That's my normal.

Some friends (who are no longer friends but something I don't yet understand) say that I don't *want* to be happy. I would love to feel at peace and be able to be my true self. In fact, next month, if all goes according to my Louise Hay affirmations, I'm going to a Pirate Weekend to learn how to be a ship captain and aggressively take over another boat.

Sure, I'm terrified—this rage is rising inside of me, a mix of an awakening greed for gold and symptoms of scurvy. Is this me? Am I a pirate? More will be revealed.

Anyhoo. I love you. And I can say that, now that we're out of the insane dance we were in.

(I've also attached an invoice—I'm learning to value my work, and so please remit one thousand dollars, payable to Bamfooco, Inc., for this letter to the editor, within ninety days, after which I will serve you a notice of collections in small-claims court.)

Agape,

ANONYMOUS
(AS WRITTEN BY MARIA BAMFORD)
LOS ANGELES, CA

DEAR McSWEENEY'S,

I am writing to you from a house in the gated Spanish Oaks community in Las Vegas, solid in my solitude, going on day fifty of quarantine. It is late April. Three years ago, I came to Las Vegas for the inaugural Believer Festival. It was one of the most wonderful literary festivals I'd ever been to, held in the sweeping Red Rock Canyon and various local venues. In front of an audience, I read a flash fiction piece as the magnificent dusk spread over the mountains behind me. I danced with Miranda July and Carrie Brownstein, met ZZ Packer, and crawled into a pink marble bathtub with a golden swan spout one night in the penthouse suite of the El Cortez Hotel, the same suite where the video for Ellie Goulding's "On My Mind" was filmed. It feels like a memory of a fever dream, especially now, during this extreme isolation.

In early March, I took a trip to Mexico for my birthday. While I was there, the pandemic was declared. Because I'd been traveling, I had to find a safe place to quarantine away from my family. At first, I thought about staying put in Mexico. Then the US announced that all Americans abroad must return immediately, and my friend urged me to get on the first flight back to the States. But to where? California was already locked down, and I had let my eighty-one-year-old grandmother take my bedroom so she could distance from the rest of my household. She usually shares a room with my cousin, who is still going into work at a bank to provide essential services.

I spent some time in a haze trying to figure out how to safely return to the US and where I should go. In the midst of this scramble, I thought: For poetry, I have put so much on hold—settling down, permanence, housing—and it's now starkly clear how fragile this life is. I travel often for gigs—my only source of income besides teaching the occasional online class or workshop; I was on the road for more than half of last year.

The day before I had to book a flight to god-knows-where, I had a conversation with Helena de Groot for her Poetry Foundation podcast, *Poetry Off the Shelf*. I expressed my regrets and pain about these life choices. I spoke about how often I had to move for this fellowship or that reading, how in the end this life did not feel sustainable, how I was now stranded because I had not put down roots. Because I had chosen poetry, I did not have the option to return home. Or at least that's what I felt in my heart, the loneliness of the wandering poet's life—how it falls apart, especially in the face of this pandemic.

Then a few things happened at the last minute. Joshua Wolf Shenk, the director of the Black Mountain Institute, which hosts the Believer Festival, read my (rather distressed) tweets about my situation and got in touch. The very literary organization that had hosted me for a book festival years ago now had an unoccupied house in Spanish Oaks for visiting writers, which it offered me as emergency housing. I was able to safely move in and, since then, I have been quarantining completely alone. In the end, after cursing my decision to become a poet on a national podcast about poetry, I had secured this emergency housing *because* I chose poetry. The narrative shifts: *because* of my choice to become a poet, I have accumulated not just this home but so many others that have become a part of my identity.

In my life I have moved about twenty times. My first move was across the hemisphere, when I was five, from the city of Wuhan, in China, to Boston—way before I ever decided to become a poet. A few decades later, for first time in my life, the city where I was born has become a household name here in the United States. And not for the reason I had hoped. Now people hear "Wuhan" and immediately think: Blame. Bats. Virus. Contamination. I wish I could paint a picture of Wuhan that is more than conspiracy theories about virology labs, wet markets, and cover-ups. But in this time of panic, that's what the discourse of this administration has devolved into: the China virus. Never mind that most of the community spread in the United States originated in Europe. It brings to mind the time when Chinese and Asian immigrants were subjected to humiliating medical procedures at Angel Island, to prove that they were not carriers of disease.

Many of my father's classmates from university are frontline ER doctors, and some of them passed away fighting the virus in Wuhan hospitals in January and February. The consequences of this pandemic—the sheer endurance of our medical communities, the solidarity of people taking collective responsibility for one another's lives—have been on my mind since the virus first appeared. Back in February, the stigma associated with Wuhan was heating up even in China. Many Wuhanese, stranded in other parts of China when the lock-down took effect, were turned away at hotels simply because of where they were from.

I can't help but feel that people from the centers of other outbreaks have not been similarly ostracized. That people's blame is directed at one place, one people. That the virus always has a Chinese face, an image stoked by politicians and celebrities alike. Recently, our racist president deflected Chinese American journalist Weijia Jiang's question with "Don't ask me. Ask China that question, okay?" On practically the same day, singer Bryan Adams posted on Instagram: "thanks to some fucking bat eating, wet market animal selling, virus making greedy bastards, the whole world is now on hold."

I find that the pain of not belonging is not something that's easily solved—and I fear, at times, that it will always remain a conundrum. Other times, though, I insist upon hope. For example, I am reminding myself right now that I am writing to you from an oasis in a desert full of dreams, in a house that poetry brought me to, through the kindness of a community of writers and artists. Without this hope, I would be truly stranded.

If this pandemic teaches me anything, it's that small acts of welcome, of caring, flourish in exceptional circumstances. I think of Wuhan, how people crowded the hospitals bringing food and supplies to their loved ones. How my people took care of one another, facing the painful onslaught of death and illness. And how now, in New York and across the world, that generosity remains true every day.

I am grateful that kindness is not always a mirage.

Yours, a poet,

SALLY WEN MAO
LAS VEGAS, NV

DEAR McSWEENEY'S,

I cut my finger earlier today slicing carrots into uneven matchstick shapes, and the result is that I am going to write to you about memory.

Moments before I cut my finger, I said to myself, "I hope I don't cut my finger." That's often how bad things happen to me. Moments before, I'll think something, and then *boom*, that something will come into being. Sometimes it's a worst-case scenario—like when I dozed off at the wheel late one night and whispered, "Wow. Be careful or you'll drive right off the road," and then, at the next turn, I again dozed off and drove right off the road—and sometimes it's not worst-case at all; it's more like a mid- or low-case scenario, which are possibly more dangerous because those are the "Be careful"s most likely to stack up without me noticing and then suddenly I'm just an unmeasured almanac of prescience and bad luck.

Here's an example. Once, long ago, let's say something like twenty or thirty or exactly thirty-two years ago, I was a child, eight years old. (I like to say things like "decades ago" to keep my age a mystery, so that my accomplishments and failures can't be measured accurately, but my bandaged-up fingertip is throbbing, so I feel like it's a good time to try being more honest and vulnerable in my writing.)

It's worth noting that I have a poor memory except for the bad things, which I remember in vivid detail. The good things are either forgotten entirely or smudged into one amorphous and hardly true beauty. Take my hometown, for example. I grew up in a poor yet prettily rural village in "Margaret Thatcher's England," which is a line I stole from the movie *Billy Elliot*, but it's the movie's fault for stealing my backdrop. We left there when I was young (but not so young that I get a pass for not forming meaningful and accurate memories), and the things I think I remember about it usually turn out to be quite untrue when I go back to visit. Entire fields just don't exist, and, yeah, in some cases they've been cleared and small stucco homes built in their places, but sometimes I realize that landmarks I'd held dear were somehow just imagined, invented.

Similarly, I don't remember ever really being parented, in the sense that I don't recall my parents saying things like *Be careful or you'll trip*, or *Be careful or you'll hit a bump on your new BMX bicycle and flip completely over the handlebars*, or *Be careful or you'll show up to school with snot on your face and then for years (or it could just be one day; that part is irrelevant) be known as "that snot-nosed Dixon girl,"* or *Be careful or you'll never remember any of this*. I don't remember their guiding voices. I know those warnings either had to have been so loud and unavoidable that they became my own internal dialogue or they weren't there at all and I filled in the gaps myself, a self-made helicopter child.

So back to that thirty-two-years-ago moment. This memory is a bad one, which is why I remember the details that matter but mess up some of the more cinematic, contextualizing parts—the parts that would occupy the richest but most skimmable pages in a book—which are all purloined and patchworked from other memories. Golden light in summer; the kind of day that stretched until 10 p.m.; gnats in my face alone; trying to keep up with my sister, who's quiet and tall; at the edge of the village's boundary, just farms and sheds and our small houses, some cows; an old man called Jack who tended the animals or maybe the sheds; wildflowers we called stickies because we could pick them and stick them to our sleeves, our backs, each other; birds overhead coming in to roost, starlings and pigeons; beauty. A jump rope, or maybe just skipping. Gravel or maybe dirt or maybe unmaintained road. My sister too far ahead, a steep downhill, scree like marbles beneath small feet in smooth rubber-soled plimsolls, and I thought (or perhaps I didn't), I can't keep up with her; I am going to fall; be careful. And then I did.

With my knee split an inch open, in an almond shape, my sister and I hobbled back to our house. I don't think she said anything to me. The only trustworthy memory I have here is of this detail: my fingertips splayed loosely across the bloody wound, like when I watch a scary movie and want to cover my face but still kind of want to see. I wanted to do something, to cover the wound, but I didn't want to touch anything gooey and sinewy or make anything worse. Jack, the old man, walked past us and nodded, English old man–style, and said something that I thought I'd never forget but it seems I have forgotten. It went something like *That looks bad*, or *You've got a bad cut, lass*, and I do remember how he didn't stop to help or walk us back to my parents. Maybe he did.

I still have a thick, raised, thirty-two-year-old scar to remember it by, but its thunder is stolen by other scars from other falls and other warnings I gave myself. *Be careful; this might be bad.*

I'm telling you this now so that you and I will always remember that the carrot matchsticks were delicious.

Love,

JULIA DIXON EVANS
SAN DIEGO, CA

WETUMPKA

by MARIA ANDERSON

I MET HIM AT the drinking fountain. He was wearing purple shorts and a sleeveless shirt with sweat mooning beneath his neck.

"How are you?" I said.

"Minding *my* own business," said William. A week later, he retained my services.

Ours was a seniors cruise, seventy-plus and gloriously understaffed, which allowed me to supplement my salary by companioning the people on board. We called them cones because you had to swerve to avoid them in the halls before they got their sea legs. Some retired on these ships. Cheaper than assisted. Here there was not much assistance available, though. If a person was prone to episodes or strokes, I boned up on what to do. Don't get me wrong. Lot of folks on the cruise, healthy as horses. Mainly I was there for company, but companioning meant I was also a sort of first responder for my cone. Except I was a woman who was awful at emergencies, intimacy, and the sort of human botany required to tend to people looking back on their lives. I needed the money for my daughter, who was in prison.

After work I'd come find him at our pool. The place was meant to resemble a sort of isolated grotto, but during the day this was the most crowded pool on board. It was only when the sun went down that we had to ourselves the natural stone, the palms and bromeliads and crane flowers with ragged leaves. He liked to hold my hand and I let him.

We'd sit disrupting the decent people.

He had elided any remaining family duties, quit contact, and left to live out the twilight of his life poolside. We spoke about auric communication, the thousand heads of the ego, tantric eating, and power leaks. He told me about the Vedic astrologer he consulted through Skype; his son, who worked for big pharma and was therefore dead to him; and his wife, who was physically dead.

"She'd wear swimsuits tighter than a gnat's asshole stretched over a rain barrel," he'd say with great reverence.

Blurry from a long day in the engine room, I'd try to listen with my whole heart. The water was calm. Pink clouds dragged themselves through the sky. A few stragglers doggy-paddled around the pool, glancing up at us every now and then.

If crew members passed by, I'd slip my hand from his. William would grin.

When he fell asleep, I'd wheel him to his cabin. Other cones I'd lift into bed, but he didn't want that. I'd wake him and he'd climb in himself. All he wanted was to know he'd made it back, so no one saw him forget himself. The sea outside his cabin windows looked like a chunk of blue anyone could come up with. At rest, his eyes remained a little open. He reminded me of a painting I'd seen at some museum, with my last cone, of an infant meditating in a hayfield.

Liner this big, we oilers had to do all sorts of stuff. Mainly I was responsible for the boilers and engines. You know the water's never actually boiling in a boiler? Equipment needed lubrication, filtration, purification. Ejectors were hell. The ejectors especially you needed to be awake to handle. Some days I checked off equipment I only thought I'd looked at, but days like today I lied in the logs, knowing I hadn't looked at something. The systems were such that you could let things go for quite a while with nothing serious happening.

We also had to clean the filters of all the pools on board, a process called backwashing, which is as rough as it sounds. More than once I had to scrape a melted adult diaper out of a heat vent. William told me this was great for cutting off a few of the thousand heads of the ego. He loved the thousand heads. He said no matter how old you got, you were still chopping off those heads.

I knew I was no better than anyone else, having raised a child on whom a lot of well-meaning people had spent a lot of money to get litigated and into her little room at Wetumpka—which, my daughter informed me, is the indigenous Muskogee word for tumbling water. I knew I wasn't any better than anyone, and still, anytime I started to think I was something special after all, there would be another adult diaper waiting for me.

Most of us oilers were from Honduras or Ecuador or El Salvador, a couple fellow Americans, all loyal folks who sent all they earned home. Seemed to me they were trading their time for nothing, because they never saw where their money went. Maybe this was easier for them because they were religious. They were already used to stuff they couldn't see.

Maybe they appreciated me because I guess in a way I wasn't seeing my money put to use either. I spent barely anything, apart from going to crew bar so people didn't start thinking I was some sort of cretin. Everything at crew bar was a buck except for a few items. Mostly, though, I abstained in favor of alone time in a storage room I'd permanently borrowed the key to, doing what I did to smooth myself out—my other expenditure. I quit officially a few months ago, after a cone of mine had a heart attack I was unprepared for. Tell you what: it took me long enough to get here. I didn't used to care about my body or what I was doing to it. But when I saw her foaming up, I said to myself, Hey, you gotta start taking care of your body, so you'll be in one piece when your girl gets out. I said, Let's give this shit up before all the foam in you starts to come out too.

If I saw my kid again, out in the world, I bet I could give it up on the spot. Even she'd left off with the powder—she wasn't inside two months before they got her straight as a stick.

But it's so lonesome here, even with Marta, my girlfriend, and I'm so tired, I need just a little, little bit. Just to get through. If I wasn't here, I'd get a dog, German shepherd, like we had growing up. But you can't have a dog here. Every morning what I want most is to give it up. But working all day with the boilers and then sitting with William's hand mashing into mine, trying to make indecent conversation and listen to someone who is not so good at making conversation or listening? I need to get back to me. I need to give something to myself. This is all I want, even when I don't want to want it. Sometimes I think there's a child in me, same as my daughter, asking for what she wants, and it's like being a mom all over again except to myself—I never know when I should say no and when I should say yes. So, after a long day, even if that morning I wrote myself a note to keep in my pocket saying, "Today I won't," after a long day, before I go meet William by our grotto, I open up that storage room door and take my little stash out and admire how I've stacked the baggies neatly, shaken the contents to the bottom right corners. I give myself some, a simple contribution.

At our grotto one muggy evening, I was saying to William how it disgusted me to see people choosing between snorkeling with dolphins and swimming with crocodiles, when my daughter couldn't even choose what she wanted for dinner. I'd seen dolphins getting boners and trying to hump women. Or worse, they picked someone to ignore, which my last cone found very hurtful—traumatizing, even.

"How do you go about swimming with a crocodile?" he said.

They had these tubes they sank into the water with people inside, so you could look the crocodiles in the eye. "It's supposedly a spiritual experience," I said. "Makes you remember a time when we were prey, before we chose to copy predators and hunt for ourselves."

Of course, my daughter does deserve to be there. But it was a system put her in there. You know? She was a child. She was a little girl. And now she is inside, and will miss the most important parts of her life, unless I earn enough money to get her some Baba Yaga of the justice system, someone who could get anyone out of anything.

William lay back on his lounger in our grotto, his faithful wheelchair beside him, and ran his hands through his hair, awaiting our entrance to the Mediterranean. This the cruise marked with waste-of-money fireworks, which give up clouds of sulfurous smoke.

"Beautiful," he murmured. If he noticed I was on something, he never said anything about it.

I wasn't that tired, just my eyes were. They kept drooping and fuzzing up. But I wasn't complaining. The only real unpleasant thing was his hand on mine, which wasn't even a dangerous or bad hand. It was just a hand—a hand that knew what the situation between us was. Sometimes I even closed my eyes and pretended it was my daughter's hand.

Crew members recycled plastic champagne flutes. They hosed burned artillery shell fireworks and other trash off the deck and into the sea. The cones liked to see us recycling, but when we docked, everything went to the same place. William and I lay quietly, the only ones there, watching the stars move inside the pool as the ship surged ahead. We had a good view of folks leaving the ship's bars and restaurants and heading to their cabins.

"Everyone here is the same shape," William remarked, watching a couple of big cones wobbling back from the bar.

Some days William would be shitting through the eye of a needle and I'd give him a teeny pill from my stash. Mostly he was healthy as a weed. Our exercise routine included swimming laps, if you could call that exercise, which I believe you could. Sure, he had the wheelchair, but the man could climb out of that thing and go. He told me he once swam a hundred miles and I believed him. He breathed through his nose when he came up for air—more efficient, he said—but mine was so wrecked from my habit I had to go mouth open. I hated how swimming made me feel. My heart would get to beating off its tracks, especially if I'd gone heavy in the storage room that week, but I enjoyed the feeling of bending and unbending my knees to propel myself forward. Plus it was good for me.

At certain points the process deepened dramatically, and I'd pass through a sort of wormhole, where everything became easier.

My girl wrote me emails with everything spelled wrong. Your mom tells you teachers are egomaniacs, of course you're going to spell everything wrong! I wanted to go back and make the opposite of every choice I ever made when it came to my daughter.

I remember when I went to see her, the pens they had in the lobby were all wobbly, like someone about to cry.

"Meal trays too," she'd said, when I remarked on this.

But I hadn't been to see her in years. I didn't want to take time off to see her again in her current condition. I'd rather make the money to get her free, so we could spend all the time together we wanted.

*　*　*

The first time I saw Marta, my girlfriend and my only friend on board besides William, we were somewhere close to Gibraltar. She had a mop out, but she wasn't mopping. She was sitting with her back to me on the other side of the pool, mop lying next to her with its hair in the water. Her hands were covering her face. She was rawboned, with a brutal chest. I wanted to sit down and cover my face too. I thought about trying to hold both of this woman's breasts in one hand, which would be impossible, and giving her a word that would be like an altar, where we could both take our sadness and lay it down as an offering. She had a face like my sister's, and I didn't even have a sister. I thought about going down to comfort her, telling her not to worry about mopping because tonight it would storm. The deck would be washed clean. Her shoulders shook and she took her hands from her face. She barked. She'd been laughing.

Marta had a mom and a brother in prison, and she hoped they never got out. She sent them postcards so they'd know what a decent, luxurious living she was making. She told them she was a performer, but she was just a janitor. Her cunt smelled like dryer sheets.

"He's paying you to make it look like you guys are fucking," Marta was saying. "Cones always need to let everyone know their pricks still work."

We were lying on her bed, naked under the covers, beneath her roommate's bunk. Marta had postcards ready to mail to her family stuck between the slats.

"Oh, come on," I said, looking up at the medieval villages of Montenegro. "People need to be touched. It's good for them. You're just jealous I'm spending time with him."

"Psh," she said. "Come out tonight."

"I need to save money," I said. Every buck counted.

"Yeah," she said gently. "But you haven't even called a lawyer yet. Have you?"

"No," I said. "I'm waiting until I have enough saved."

"You don't even know what enough is," she said. "Plus, there's no way she's getting out. Right?"

Honestly? She wasn't, no. But you never knew.

I'd thought of moving to Alabama to be near my girl, but I felt reluctant to spend all this money I was saving. Plus, where would I work? Would I remember how to drive a car? There seemed to be vast quantities of new, impossible technology you had to learn in order to function.

William and I lay by our pool. He'd brought a bag of popcorn and we practiced what he called tantric eating. According to him, the act of eating was a consecrated part of spiritual evolution. He'd charge the food by whispering a blessing over it from his astrologer, and we'd have to eat very slowly, focusing on extracting the essence. As the kernels dissolved on my tongue, I watched a few pool tiles wiggling, which felt like the tiles of my body underneath my skin, twitching from the maintenance bumps I'd done half an hour ago. Two linebackery women in matching black Hawaiian shirts walked past. Dark Hawaii: an especially popular fashion trend for cones.

I was tired of living inside my tiles.

And I didn't think he asked to hold my hand because he wanted people to know his dick still worked. I think what William wanted was the oldest thing, what people have wanted since the beginning of time: to belong, to connect.

Then again, I have a certain look, which throughout my life has taught me that everyone—most people—do want to sleep with me. I'm not being stuck-up. I'm saying they want to use my face and my body to get off. There's nothing to be proud of about this, which is something people really misunderstand. It is not a compliment when someone wants to fuck you.

But these black-Hawaiian-shirt women. They wore gift-shop monkeys around their handsome, fat necks. Velcro-stripped paws. The monkeys looked as though they were using these women as transport and might strangle them after. They had long, thin arms. They'd hold on for decades if no one bothered them, until the Velcro failed. The women laughed, and I knew that even if they weren't laughing at me, they would laugh at me, if they knew my situation. It was a laughable life I was living. I imagined one ripping the other's monkey off in a few minutes to suck her face.

"Sisters or boning?" I said.

"Sisters," he said. I noticed them notice us in the dark. You always hear about creepy men watching women from the bushes, but more often I'm the creep watching. One woman pointed at us and said something I couldn't hear, and they both laughed again. William rubbed my palm with his thumb. His hand was a croissant damp from a greasy bag, and I pressed into it, feeling the soft skin depress over muscle.

William drifted off to sleep, but I stayed by the pool, too tired to get up.

When my third-grade teacher began inviting me to his condo's communal sauna, we used it as if it were the most solitary and ordinary place in the world. I wasn't in third grade anymore by then. I was a junior in high school. But the middle and high school were connected by a little bridge, and I'd taken to having lunch with him in his classroom while we tried to fix his boiler. When he slept with me in his sauna, he told me it was because I was luscious and he'd always wanted me, ever since I was in his class, and that he needed me, and we had a marvelous time, the most beautiful time I'd had so far with a man, until later I thought back on the sauna and the lunches and realized I didn't know anything, that I'd misunderstood nearly everything he did and everything I did. I'd gotten it all badly out of context, and this sensation started to live inside me, the feeling that anything I thought I knew, I was actually getting awfully wrong. I began to see doom everywhere. Anything good could be the worst thing to happen to you. So when my daughter went inside, I thought, Maybe here is a good thing, instead of another bad thing come along. Anything good seemed bad anyway. Anything bad seemed good. Did it really matter? Couldn't you just designate one thing as the other, and the logic would fall into place? My senior year, I'd fuck the man who would become my daughter's father in a sauna, thinking not pleasantly of my third-grade teacher and what he'd done to me.

In my more positive moments I thought, What is life anyway but a series of rooms, one as good as the other? I had a roommate who snipped her nails on her top bunk so they fell onto mine, a kind of bodily confetti. Not as bad as having to sleep in a room where the lights never went off, where the temperature was kept cold to prevent germs from spreading. My daughter was reading books. She'd told me plenty in her emails about what she did in there, the food, her friends, the courts, the laundry room where she worked, same as she had on the outside. She was studying toward a graphic design degree.

On the phone one day she told me she'd started tattooing at Wetumpka, which was making her quite popular and earning her commissary besides.

"What are the sanitary procedures?" I said.

"I burn the needles," she said.

Everyone in there wanted a tattoo, according to her. Made me think of her dad, who always told her she looked like a school desk someone had scribbled all over. I personally thought she looked like the back of a church pew, where the Bic pen carvings were precise and seemed to involve a lot of effort and redoing to get the lines so deep. What I mean is, I believe my daughter's markings were not how they looked—haphazard, procured in a boozy haze—but were her way of articulating her destiny. She'd repeated the markings as many times as she needed throughout her life because she was a repetitive, solemn, reverent girl, and always had been.

"It's great," she said. "No one wants to hurt the tattoo girl."

In my more negative moments I remembered all the incompetent drawings my daughter had done as a kid. I didn't ask how someone who couldn't draw had picked up tattooing, but obviously a mother worries.

I called up a lawyer that evening. I told the woman how much money I had saved. The lawyer sounded like Martha Stewart, which struck me as a good thing because though Martha was overindulgent and lazy, she was savvy enough to turn her jail stint into a cooking show with Snoop Dogg, which has always seemed to me like awfully smart marketing.

What the fuck is white pepper, he'd say, or something like that.

She'd go, *Snoop, I couldn't agree with you more.*

"Tell you what," the lawyer said to me. "I'll look into it and give you a buzz back."

Weeks went by. I never heard from her.

William and I were both advocates of routine. Mornings when I had time before work, we'd do our swim in the grotto pool, William ahead of me in his tiny purple shorts. I swam in my uniform top and a pair of men's striped running shorts with a mesh dick pocket I liked, a place for the organ and balls I did not have.

Everything had a place, I thought. My daughter had a place at Wetumpka, which was reassuring in a way. I had a place in my fingernail bed. William had a place at the pool and in his cabin.

His quads were stunning, the only place on his body without wrinkles. He swam daily out of a restlessness that seemed to propel him in all things.

"Come on, come on, come on!" William would say as we swam lap after lap, and when he said it I could do it.

People would smile at us from their loungers, at the thirtysomething woman struggling behind the older man. At first I'd be faster, but after a few laps he'd move ahead for good. I'd be behind him, my heart wiggling in my chest and my lungs throbbing.

After, William would climb up into his wheelchair and I'd wheel him around. One morning we passed one of the gift-shop monkeys curled like a squashed spider in a corner. We passed a row of women applying temporary tattoos of glittered hibiscuses to their arms. We passed Marta wheeling a cleaning cart and I felt like someone had opened the bathroom door while I was pissing. I wanted to know what William thought of Marta. I was tempted to tell him who she was to me, but I was too embarrassed by her large breasts, by how her legs were long, featureless sticks below a cute pooched belly. I didn't have anyone else who would give me an outside perspective on her, not even my roommate, who, apart from the fingernails, shared the room like you'd share a seat with a stranger on a bus.

"How'd your daughter end up in prison, anyway?" he asked as I pushed him.

I wasn't entirely sure what my girl had done to get into Wetumpka and I told him so. I'd kept out of the court stuff and she hadn't wanted to worry me. She'd shot someone, a robbery gone wrong, drugs. She'd chosen earwigs for friends. That's all I got. Every unintended murder's pretty much the same, isn't it. Someone says, "Oops," and everything goes very quickly to shit.

Nights when new crew boarded, everyone, even me, went to crew bar to scope out the new employees, to think about making a move on someone before repeat offenders pounced. At home I'd been the one you got warned about. Here people I barely spoke to warned me about Marta. I sat in the corner, thinking of William in his lounger next to our grotto. I watched Marta buy dollar margaritas for a new woman who was offensively tiny, with infant arms, wearing a disgusting outfit, high-waisted pants and a shirt that showed her flat gut. I would like to be the type of woman who wouldn't stand for this—Marta hitting on someone else in front of me—but if I'm being honest, I'm not. I don't not stand for anything anymore.

Another oiler came up and talked to me, which was rare. He wanted to tell me how Marta slept with cones for money. I shrugged. He went back to his people.

I peeled a label off a ginger beer and watched my non-acquaintances, folks I never wished to know, move their mouths and grow softer and more animated. Marta was next to me again. I'd shifted to real beer even though I didn't drink anymore and soon she was sitting beside me. We went to her room.

Her roommate was reading on the top bunk, holding a slap-full glass of tea on her chest, but we were used to her and argued like we were alone.

From Marta's face you'd think she'd be fat, but she was very thin, except, of course, for the tits, and the tiny belly she had from drinking. The transition between face and body was arousing: you took in the face and forced your eyes down, correcting what you thought you were seeing. It was the correcting that got me.

"I saw you the other day," she said. "Holding hands with William It's weird,"

"I retained a lawyer," I told her.

"You did not," she said.

"Well, I called one."

"And? Can he get her out?"

"It's a she," I said, "and we're going to try."

"Uh-huh," she said.

"You ever sleep with a cone?" I said.

"Of course not." She frowned at me.

If you got caught coning, you were toast, and you had to pay for your flight home from whichever port was next. I'd rather die than risk getting fired.

*　　*　　*

A few days later, when I kept pressing her, she changed her story. "Oh, on Disney," she said. "Everyone does on Disney. Here's different."

"You slip them the Mickey?" I said. An old joke. Disney cruises were known for harassment and date rape among the employees. Plus pervs signed on to be around kids.

"You think your daughter deserves to go free?"

"She's my kid," I said. "Of course I do."

"Look, I'm telling you this out of love. She's not getting out," said Marta. "You're delusional. I used to think it was helping you, believing you could make enough to get her free. But you've got to let yourself leave her behind. It's like you won't get off this ship because it would mean you'd have to face her being stuck in there."

I didn't say anything.

"I'm leaving," she said. "I'm going home. You should too."

We sat there a long time. I was looking up at a postcard of some moonlit waterfall in Cyprus, thinking of the bullshit she'd send me about her new life. All she needed to be happy about her life was someone to lie to about how good it was. I envied her for that.

Next port, Marta left for good. I called a million lawyers. They all said they'd email me soon as possible. They said I had enough funds to get started. They explained what getting started was, but it didn't sound like much.

I was on my way to see William, late from repairing a three-hour engine room mistake, after whaling on what I had in the storage room because I was crashing, doing more every day just to stay awake, when a tall, beer-bellied cone stopped me and called me honey and put his hand on my neck and demanded to see the captain. This happens all the fucking time. Plastered people always want to see the captain. They want to meet the person guiding the vessel. They begin to understand this is their right.

The man was pregnant with a lifetime's worth of beer, his skinny legs shaking.

"Let go of me or I'll push you overboard," I hissed. "Want to find out how it feels to hit the water from ninety feet?"

He grabbed my arm. "Lemme see him, dyke," he said. I smelled like grease from the boilers. I felt smudged. The man caught my other arm and grinned. I kneed him in the balls, stomped his Crocs. He grinned wider and held on.

"Take me," he said, "to the motherfucking captain."

All I could think of was my daughter in similar situations, locked in embraces with women who don't have to worry about sunscreen for a long time, or ever again.

When I finally got to William, he crabbed his hand at me, stretching his palm and wiggling his fingers. I waited a long beat before taking hold of it.

A man nudged a rusted walker ahead of him as if it were a reluctant, beloved pet. "Come on now," the man said gently. "Come on."

"Pathetic," I said, crouching to pick a leaf off the water's surface.

"He seems sweet," said William, squeezing. "Your hand is always so sweaty." He patted it absently. "A very worried hand."

It rained while we sat there. I watched the drops hit the stone around the pool. I watched individual drops smack the palm fronds and the bromeliads and the crane flowers.

"I wish it wasn't raining," I said. I was pushing my heart along like the man with the walker. I missed Marta already.

"Power leak," he said. That's what he called any phrase that began with wishing for something different.

I told him wishing was most of my life.

"Then you're giving away all your power," he said.

My daughter had always been so thin, thin in a way that made her muscles show because there was nothing to get in the way. Unlike me, she was tough, the kind of person whose skeleton you could see right there under her face. Looking at my girl, you were reminded that beneath our face tissue and skin and all the more impermanent bits, we had no eyes or nose, not really, just holes in our skulls that, once we died, would allow bugs and bacteria to get inside our heads and help us break down into something useful again. Mouths we had; teeth, yes; but all the other face stuff was weak. Bones, on the other hand, were strong. And my girl was nothing but bone, bone, bone.

"Hey," William said. "I'm still here."

"Sorry," I said. "I was just thinking about my daughter."

The kid kept telling me she was straight. I hoped it was true. I'd heard folks stuck drugs in Nerf footballs and threw them over the walls, swallowed them during visitation, even used drones. Drones! I'd heard from a cousin inside that they'd invented this spray. You sprayed it on a letter, baked the letter in the oven to cure it, and mailed it to the inmate, who smoked the letter like weed. Paper, they called it.

When I looked back at William, he'd fallen asleep, and I wheeled him to his cabin, feeling bad for not being great company. I tried to wake him up. When he wouldn't budge, I checked his pulse—normal—and lifted him into his bed. He was light as a child.

On a port day I met up with William at a nearby beach. He had a saffron-stained tongue. He handed me his paella leftovers in a Styrofoam box like a kindly leper. I told him I wasn't swimming that day and he seemed to understand. I ate while he swam in his girly purple shorts. I pressed the shrimp between my tongue and the roof of my mouth so the juices leaked out. I followed his glistening form back and forth, hoping he wouldn't find a hidden riptide in the crowded water. You always heard about riptides, these erotic, draggy forces.

I'd seen a lifeguard put purple dye in a rip before, saw how quickly the dye flew out to sea.

When William came out of the water, his head was shiny and wet and hit with so much sunlight it was no color at all. He hobbled over and collapsed into the chair.

I was missing Marta so bad. Maybe she was right about Wetumpka. I was glad I had William.

"I don't want you to pay me anymore," I said. "I just want to be friends."

"Don't be silly," he said.

"How's your heart these days?" I said. "You wouldn't wake up last night."

He shrugged and toweled off. He rubbed his head vigorously before settling into his wheelchair.

"You don't think about someone for long enough, they disappear," said William. "And I've been trying to not think about anyone for so long."

I nodded.

"But now I've been thinking about them and they're all coming back," he said.

I stared out at the swimmers, who were hollering with joy every time a big wave came in. A young, big woman swam out past the rest, went underwater, and reappeared so far away I could no longer make out the tattoos encircling her chest and arms. She appeared one more time, glimmering in the distance, before I let her go.

At the next port, I had a message from Wetumpka. My daughter had been hospitalized. She'd been in solitary confinement for reasons they couldn't share, but somehow she'd gotten into a fight in the shower. They had no other information at this time.

William bought us both hundred-year-old ham to eat on the beach. After the ham, he handed me another Styrofoam container, this one with a honey-and-cheese dessert inside. I ate mine in two bites and he did too.

"What's the crunchy part?" I said.

"Walnuts."

He had fine grains of sand on his lips, clear like salt crystals. "Heart bothering you?" I said. He shook his head. Our hands sweated white sunscreen sweat.

Above us were a few daytime stars. We were quiet. We lay there on the sand.

"Goddammit," he said. "Goddammit all to hell."

I had to agree. I reached for his hand and he squeezed mine. Together we took in the sea.

AFTERNOONS

Comics by Jon McNaught

FUN

ESCAPE FROM
THE DYSPHESIAC
PEOPLE

by BRANDON HOBSON

BELOVED GRANDCHILDREN: DR. ESTEP has recommended I tell the story of how, many years ago, I escaped from the Darkening Land and returned home. I escaped from the men who talked funny, the ones who removed me from my home and cut my hair and put me on a train. I expected it would happen; they had already taken all my friends from school. It occurred late one night in September in what my aunt Adele referred to as the Year of Removal, when all those men from the Darkening Land Commune arrived in our small community. I won't lie: when these men broke into our house I was so terrified I couldn't speak. They were all wearing dark jackets and holding handcuffs and claiming they were from "juvenile services." Their voices were difficult to understand—I heard in them the slurred ramblings of drunkards or southerners and feared for my life. I knew stories of how they drugged people and brainwashed them to work and act in their non-indigenous ways. My poor aunt Adele went into hysterics, cursing at them, screaming in rage, and they restrained her and pulled me away. They held me down and shaved my head. The last thing I remember was one of them saying, "It's the Boys Ranch for you." Then I blacked out.

You might know that such trauma—the removal from your home, from your family, from your own identity—causes unease even after years of talking about it, and so be it, my beloved! But this is not so much a story of a traumatic event as it is a story of escape. This is not a mélange of distorted events, nor is it a call for sympathy. You must know the history of removal, and this is my own history—my way of remembering those weeks when I was gone. Holy hell. What was weeks felt like months. Dr. Estep told me some years later that my entire sense of time would be misplaced and exaggerated as I recalled all that had happened, and for a while it was. Beloved: I was only fifteen when they took me.

When I awoke I was on a train headed to the Darkening Land. One of the "juvenile services" men said I needed structure. He sat beside me and snoozed. Everyone on the train looked dead. I saw their bodies slumped, mouths open. Outside, the world flew by. I wasn't able to see anything except fog. In the window I noticed my smoky reflection. I leaned against the cold glass and tried to sleep. A man a few rows in front of me stood from his seat. His spine was so badly crooked he was bent forward, craning his neck to look back at me. He was coughing dust and smoke.

I could barely understand what was going on with the people on the train. Another older man and his wife were in seats across from me. The man's face sagged from his skull. He blew his nose into a handkerchief. "I don't feel well," he told his wife.

"You're pale," she said. "You look tired and pitiful."

"I don't feel well," he kept saying.

By the time we pulled in to the station, I felt sick too. I had the taste of battery acid in my mouth. I sat and waited while others got their bags and exited. I had my own bag, which I slung over my shoulder as I walked off the train with the "juvenile services" officer. He led me by the arm through the lobby to a pale man who wore glasses that magnified his eyes in a very sinister way. He squinted at me as I approached. I realized there were people all around, watching us.

"Ah, we'll go to the car," the man said, and led me by the arm. Everyone led me by the arm, as if I were a small child. It was irritating and worrisome. This man talked funny. I would've made a run for it, but my legs were heavy and sore from the long train ride, plus there were officers all around. The pale man led me outside to a parking lot. It was still dark out, but I knew the sun would be coming up soon. When we reached the car, the man stopped and turned to me.

"I was stabbed in a public toilet," he told me. He pulled up his shirt and showed me a mass of scars in his side. "I won't tell you the details, son. Ah. It happened at a restroom in a park. The guy thought I wanted to lie with him for sexual explorations or experimentations and penetrations. But I just needed to pee. Ah. He stabbed and robbed me."

I didn't know what I was supposed to say.

"Mah," he said. "Forget what I said about penetrations. It's safe on the ranch. You won't get stabbed. Ah, you'll have your own room. We're all dysphesiac, so bear with us. Ah."

He twitched as he spoke. We got into his car, a battered thing smelling of rotting food and cigarette smoke. He puckered his lips and lit a cigarette, then started the engine and asked what music I wanted to listen to. His smoke hung in the air.

I remained silent.

He pulled out of the lot and turned up the radio, but there was no music. I heard static, only static.

On the drive, the pale man told me his name was Jackson. We drove through winding streets lined with barren trees, past a tall grain elevator and empty buildings. There were deserted motels with shattered windows and broken signs. Empty parking lots, trash strewn on the streets. A dense fog hung on the horizon like smoke. The boardinghouse we arrived at was a brick two-story with a large front porch and a flickering yellow porch light. The yard was full of weeds. Like the rest of the town, the neighborhood was silent and dead. I decided right then that I wouldn't like it. In Jackson's yard I saw the ancient tree with cracked bark that resembled the faces of the dead. Insects crawled all over it, buzzing, twitching their antennae.

I followed Jackson into the rotting house and asked for water to drink. The living room was warm and bare, with a few paintings on the walls of tanks and aircraft. I noticed model airplanes around the room—on the TV, on shelves, and one in pieces on the dining room table, which Jackson silently pointed to as we walked past. He showed me my room, in the back, with a single bed and a window that looked out on the backyard. A desk fan was on and hummed quietly. I lay down on the bed.

"I'll be back with a glass of mmmwater," Jackson said.

I kicked off my shoes and closed my eyes. When I opened them he was there again, standing over me with the glass.

"Drink this," he said. He sat on the edge of the bed. "There will be work for you to do here. Ah."

I shook my head.

"Mah," he said. His face twitched. "You'll choose your name, son. How about Jim? Think about it, ah, or maybe we'll just call you Chief."

"I don't want to change my name," I said.

"Chief it is. Oh, ah, you'll need to learn to act and talk just like us."

I shook my head.

"Mah," he said. "Your hair looks good short. You're in better territory, ah, away from the dusty plains. Away from the tornadoes and the rattlesnakes. You'll be happier here. Oh. Ah."

He twitched and talked for a long time about sickness and loneliness and displacement, but I don't remember everything he said. He was a sad, angry man with a long face. I have seen cattle whose faces reminded me of this man's. When he was finished talking he told me goodnight and left. But I was unable to fall asleep, unsure of my exact location. I knew I was somewhere in the middle, maybe the Midwest, nowhere near the plains. The train went east and north, it seemed. Outside it was still dark. I tried to concentrate on something peaceful: an open field at dusk, a big sky.

I heard barking outside and got up to look out the window. I saw hounds rummaging around, tearing into garbage. One of the hounds ran off with something in its mouth. The others were fighting, growling and barking at one another. I saw dark trees with low-drooping branches. I saw black vultures hanging in the moonlit sky.

Now this happened: At some point I woke in the middle of the night, confused. It took a moment to remember where I was, my surroundings. I saw the glass of water on the nightstand beside me. My bag and my shoes were on the floor. I sat up and saw the figure of an old man standing in the doorway, an apparition. I didn't recognize him. His hair was silver and long and hung languidly.

I was too afraid to say anything, and after a moment he turned and left. I got up and followed him. He walked into the bathroom, where he looked at his reflection in the mirror. He raised his hands to touch the mirror, tilted his head, studying himself. I could see his reflection, but it was much blurrier than he appeared in the room. I reached and turned on the light, but as soon as I did he disappeared. I turned the light off and on again, but he didn't reappear. "Where are you?" I whispered. I called for him, but he never responded. I turned and walked through the quiet house, in the dark, looking for him. I peeked into a bedroom and saw Jackson asleep with his back to me, snoring. His room hummed with a fan.

I stepped quietly back to the bathroom. Again, I turned the light on and off, whispered for him, then returned to my bedroom. From the window, I saw a hawk resting on a fence post at the back of the yard. The hawk was still while the moon shone blue in the dark sky. I sat on the bed and glanced at the clock; it was almost four in the morning.

What was I supposed to think? I wasn't able to go back to sleep, too unsettled by what I had witnessed, too afraid of whatever it meant.

Beloved: I saw many people that first night. Apparitions of women and men with blankets over their shoulders, walking down the hallway. I saw children being carried. I saw people crawling and reaching out to me for help. They kept coming and coming, walking and crawling down the hallway past my bedroom. In the dark I couldn't see their faces, but their bodies were struggling against a wind, pushing forward. My ancestors, I thought. My ancestors walking the Trail.

I stared into the dark hall. I felt compelled to watch them. They pushed forward and kept walking, falling. Soon enough, I began to nod off, but all night I kept waking to images of bodies in the hall. People crying out, walking, crawling. I saw a woman approach me. She brought me a seed basket with good cause. She was very beautiful, slender with long raven hair.

"I'm planting pink cherry blossoms to swell in the gray-world," she told me. "The Seven Dancers, the Pleiades star system, is our home. Follow the road out and remember the Tsalagi is about harmony." Smoke drooled from her mouth as she walked away.

After that I drifted in and out of sleep until the room brightened. I woke horrified and knew I had to leave the place. I knew I needed to find a way to get out of that house. I lay in bed and thought of Aunt Adele back home. I missed her terribly. I thought of my dead ancestors whose spirits roamed the land, whose celestial forms moved in all different directions, who entered the bodies of bobcats and eagles or floated aimlessly with the wind. I thought of the ones sitting silent on the mountains, watching the trees sway with the blowing snow, their images disappearing into the whiteness.

I rose and went into the living room, where a man introduced himself as Andrew Jack's son, Carl. He was a giant who stood so tall his head nearly reached the ceiling. He wore a green cap and overalls and was eating a piece of chicken while reading a newspaper. He had flocculent hair and a puckered face. He spoke in a deep voice, I remember.

"You're awake, boy," he said, looking down at me.

"Who is Andrew Jack?" I asked.

"My own pa," he said. "Andrew Jack is my pa, period."

I took my hands out of my pockets and crossed my arms because Carl the giant made me nervous the way he stood there eating his piece of chicken.

"I told you a story last night, boy, while you was asleep, about the sinner who doesn't work. Period. I hope it entered your subconscious, boy."

I remained silent.

"Fah," he said. "We own the whole ranch out here, period. We own the house and the barn out there, where you'll work with the other Indians we took from that town of yours, period. My job is to supervise, period, ah, the kitchen out there while Jackson supervises the field."

He seemed to be waiting for me to say something, but I didn't speak.

"Fah," he said, chewing.

I sat down and waited as he finished his chicken leg, making disgusting chewing sounds. Finally, he wiped his hands on his pants and said we'd go out to the barn to work with the others, shoveling and cleaning it up. "There's work to be done today," he said. "It's, ah, your first day here, period. Fah."

"What work?" I said.

"You'll shovel. Ah. I'm tired to the bone but you'll shovel and also carry barrels, boy. Clean the can, period. I'll mine the kitchen for the others making calf fries or fuel our vehicles unbeknownst to furlong horse dung."

"What?"

"Fah," he said, and as he grinned sinisterly at me I noticed his blistered lip.

Listen up, grandchildren: I worked that whole day with very little food. I shoveled dirt and cow- and horse shit and raked hay. I cleaned the stable with six other Indians and we weren't even allowed to talk.

At the end of the afternoon I was so weak from hunger I was bowled over from stomach pains.

And this was how it was every day for a few weeks. No school, just work. Every day we loaded and moved barrels and wheelbarrows full of rocks and dirt and vegetables from a garden. I raked dirt and rocks and shoveled horse shit. At night my arms were so sore I couldn't wash my face. They fed us every evening, but the food wasn't very good. Sometimes they let us watch the black-and-white television until nine or so, then it was off to bed. At least I had my own room, though I remember every once in a while one of the other Indian boys, Thomas, I think, would ask to sleep in my room. I never agreed.

"Mine is horrible," he said. "I have to share it with two little kids who piss the bed every night. They cry and beg to go home. Last night we watched Carl catch a rat with his bare hands; then he ate it."

"A rat?" I said.

"Carl is a monster. He's cockeyed and pale. He's a ten-foot-tall beast who opens his mouth and breathes."

I kept my head down and worked. I prayed to the Great Spirit that someone would come rescue me. While the others complained so much, I mostly kept quiet. I knew if I could just stay silent and work, maybe they wouldn't push me as hard as the others. I wrote letters to Aunt Adele and told her I missed her and that I would find a way to come home. Carl said he would mail the letters, but I don't think he ever did, because I never heard back from Aunt Adele. It made me sad, especially at night when I tried to fall asleep. Jackson felt sorry for me, I suppose, because one night he invited me to help carry the beer kegs from the back of the truck to a barn dance in town. The other boys were at a different house. I was sure glad I wasn't with them, doing whatever work they had to do there. I guess Jackson must've liked me some to let me go. I was glad to go with him, which was better than staying at the house with Carl the giant and his dad.

In town I helped Jackson load the truck, even though my arms were still hurting from the work I'd done. We drove out to the southern part of town and down a gravel road, where there were plenty of cars parked. I was glad to see that a couple of Jackson's friends were there to help move the beer kegs into the barn.

Already, at dusk, the barn was crowded. A band of old men with gray beards and straw hats played some type of old, sad country music, droning slide guitar and low singing. I became aware of my surroundings, the people around me wearing loose-fitting flannel shirts and boots. I saw the intensity and pain on people's faces, no laughter at all.

Jackson told me to stay put and stepped away a minute. While he was gone I overheard two pale men talking near me. "The jaw's sore," one guy said to the other. "Increased gun sales, people on edge. Fah. Fought Indians today."

The other guy rocked on his heels. "Let's all be mighty proud, Taggert."

"Fought in a public toilet," the first guy said, twitching. "Jah. Jaw soreness is worrisome. No comment."

"For me it's the throat. Damn the sheriff. I heard he left for good, rode off into the cherry blossoms."

"Open your mouth and let me look. Ah. Ah."

I found myself staring at them until they noticed. One of the guys gave a friendly nod, but I didn't nod back. No matter where I looked, I felt threatened. I couldn't take it. Jackson returned with an old man who was thin and pale, with a face like a badger's. He asked about how wildcat masks were used to stalk wild turkeys.

"Also," he said, his face twitching, "we understand there's a way Jim Thorpe dominated sports with his body, using his strength."

Jackson coughed into his fist. "Mah, that's all purely speculation. The boy's here to work on the ranch."

They both looked at me, waiting for a response.

I asked where the restroom was, and Jackson said I'd have to go outside. "I'll have to walk beside you," he said, and we wandered to the other side of the room, where I noticed a group of people huddled around a bunch of mannequins. All the mannequins were faceless and unclothed, as if the barn were storage for unused department store equipment. They were positioned in different poses. Some had their arms raised. Others were kneeling. Their faces had no eyes or mouths, only noses. I found myself staring at them.

"It's for pictures," Jackson said. "For the newspaper, nothing else. Ah. Don't just stand there, boy. Go ahead look at them or do you need to pee."

I went over to one of the mannequins. It was a man on his knees, crawling. He was wearing a headdress, and I knew then that he was supposed to be an Indian. I knew then that they were all supposed to be Indians. I leaned in and touched the mannequin's face. I looked at all of them in their poses, hunched, crawling, their hands reaching out for help. It was too similar to the apparitions that had appeared in the middle of the night. My ancestors, crawling, suffering, dying on the Trail. It was sickening. I felt a chill and then suddenly nauseated. People around me, all throughout the room, were glancing at me. When I looked at them they looked away.

I had been ill at ease since I'd arrived at the ranch, but now I felt the terror. It hit hard right then. This terror was unlike anything I had felt, and I knew I had to get out of there. I looked at Jackson and pointed to my stomach.

"Stomach pain," he said. "Vomit? You got to go outside."

I nodded, and he led me to the door near the back of the barn. I stepped outside and he pointed to a tree nearby, where I walked, looking back at him. He stood at the doorway, a shadow in the night. This was the last I ever saw of pale, foul-lipped Jackson.

Beloved: I ran. I ran from the barn as hard as I could, following the road heading south to a small field. I could see the main street on the other side of the field. Squeezing my way through a large bush and a wooden fence, I ran down a small slope of grass to the dark field, where I heard things around me grunting and croaking, like frogs in a pond, but I didn't let them startle me. I would find a train, a bus, some way to get out.

I ran and ran. Bulbous clouds assumed strange shapes. The mist
hanging above the grass was dense. The road seemed to open up into
a new world, and to the east I saw the sun rising. I followed the road
as it wound around and downhill, walking now, until I saw it dead-
end ahead, past a park. Tall trees towered over the horizon, and all
around me were plum trees and peach trees and pink cherry trees. It
was a land of enchantment. Suddenly a boy on a bicycle rode by. He
rang his bicycle bell as he passed, and I watched him coast down the
hill toward a playground, where he climbed off his bicycle and ran
to a group of other kids. There was a small pond and an old house
at the end of the road. I began to walk toward them, and as I got
closer I noticed an older man working in his yard. He wore overalls,
and though I couldn't see his face I saw he had long white hair to his
shoulders. He was down on his knees, digging through a trash bag.
As I passed him, he stood and looked at me.

"Siyo," he said.

I gave a slight wave and kept walking.

"Wait a minute," he said. "Did you hear me? I said hello."

I turned and looked at him. He waved me over and told me his name
was Tsala. His eyes held an intensity, full of pain and abandonment.

"There's the road with the pink cherry blossoms," he said. He
stood with a stoop. He pointed toward the woods beyond where the
road ended, and I noticed for the first time the swollen pink blossoms. In the blue-gray world, it was the brightest color I had seen.

I followed him around to the back of his house. He invited me into
his kitchen. On the walls was thick wallpaper with flowery designs,
and ovals and rectangles where pictures used to hang. I saw dishes piled
in the sink, spilled coffee, vials and prescription bottles of pills on the
counter. There was a small kitchen table with two chairs. He sat in one
and pointed for me to sit in the other, across from him.

He poured us coffee. I drank it black from a chipped mug. I was
glad to see another Native person. He brought his pipe and we shared
a smoke. I noticed one eye was blue and the other gray. He got up

and left the room for a few minutes, and when he returned he had a handful of stones that he set on the table in front of me. He took a pencil and drew a triangle on a piece of paper and placed stones within it. He chewed on sugarcane and spoke in a low, serious voice. "These are the stones that represent the wisdom fire within you," he said. "Look for the fire."

I leaned in and studied the triangle and a stone within it. "Rose quartz," Tsala said. "For overcoming grief. You can begin healing. I want you to keep it with you. Reach into the triangle and take it."

I reached in and took the stone. I looked at it in my hand. It was rose-colored and smooth.

"Remember your ancestors," he told me. "Remember they were removed from their homes, and then they had no homes. They walked the Trail, walked and crawled and died. They suffered. But you already know this. Come with me."

Tsala led me back outside. "I have the stories that heal," he said. "All stories heal. Tell me, where is your home?"

"Oklahoma."

"Go follow this trail lined with cherry blossoms," he said. "It leads westward to a place without sadness or death or men who talk funny."

He shook my hand and I told him goodbye. As I started to walk, I turned back to him and watched him turn into an eagle, spread his wings, and fly into the gray sky.

Beloved grandchildren: I followed that trail. I escaped the Darkening Land. I walked down it and was not afraid, and I felt no worry about where I was going, which I knew was west because I could see in the distance the setting sun. The sky was turning pink and yellow. Soon white feathers were falling all around me, flooding the trail like fresh winter snow. I saw my ancestors ahead, but they were not crawling and wailing; they were standing. The winding trail I walked was lined with cherry blossoms, and I did not grow tired, and the sky opened up with the language of the elders saying: *Home.*

MEEMAW FUCKS A WOLF

by LEAH HAMPTON

WHEN THE WOLF CAME to her for the last time, many years on, Meemaw thought she could protect herself. True, she was sick. Her breasts were pocked with an inflammatory cancer that had slithered into her vital organs, and these days she spent most of her time in bed. She ate nothing but cold cornbread and honey. And, true, she had neglected to put storm windows on her cabin last winter, so with one sharp rap on the thin panes, any beast could break into the house. Late winter slushed and drizzled outside, and the drizzle often froze into slick patches of ice on her front porch and along her gravel driveway. If she stepped into one of these patches and slipped, she'd break herself—most likely her left hip, which was already a porous, weakened bone. The black ice winked and sparkled at Meemaw in the pale March sun, saying, *Try me, woman; let me take you down.* And, true, she was alone in the woods. Her daughters and grandbabies visited once a week at most. If she fell, if the wolf bested her, no one would hear her cries.

But Meemaw had her barlow knife, and arms corded with old muscle, and knowledge of the woods and March ice and the habits of beasts. She had her wits. She had an old shotgun, if it came to that. And despite her illness, she still had all her hair—fine and wavy and red—the wolf's favorite. She was past fifty now, and it had darkened to auburn, with filaments of silver that shone like needles in the lamplight. No longer the hair of a girl in desperate, new love. But still red enough for a wolf.

He would come. She was sure of it. He sensed her weakness, smelled the cancer on her from deep in the woods, and she could swear that twice now, at dawn, she had seen him lurking behind the poplars high on the ridge above her house. Black-cold eye, thick tail. These glimpses brought back thoughts of the wolf's russet fur, and the arcing sinews along his chest and stomach. Meemaw dizzied and shivered at the remembrance. The best lovers never leave us.

She had been fifteen the first time he tried to take her. Though she was only a girl then, she knew what the wolf was, because this was a time when the mountains held many such animals. She knew herself to be bright and worth saving, so she did not succumb to him. Instead she fought him off and stabbed his haunch.

"Wolf," she had told him, "I reckon I know what you come for."

She and her friends and sisters were swimming in the creek, and she stood soaked and half-dressed at the edge of the water. Behind a low shrub, she could see a panting, wet, canine mouth and black eyes darting between the girls.

Her voice was sharp and strong, a voice the other girls feared. It echoed off the stones and boulders in the creek. "You keep away."

She held her knife aloft and shouted curses into the woods.

When the other girls had gone and her back was turned for a moment, she heard a whisper of parting branches, and the wolf was upon her. He pushed her to the ground and began to tear off her damp shirt with his teeth. She lay on her stomach, her knife useless in her pocket. Pulses of light flashed behind her eyes, and all around her was the scent of pine.

"Quit it," she said, kicking her feet. "You ain't better than me."

The wolf laughed and reared up to take his first bite, and she spun on her hips in the dirt. She flipped herself over and screamed and cursed him as she pulled her knife out and sank the blade into his body.

The wolf did not yelp. Instead he gasped, and cocked his head the way dogs do, and released her. He shook his whole body, ear to tail, and sat down.

She scrambled to her feet and dusted herself off.

"Leave me alone," she said.

The wolf stretched his paws out in front of him and lay on the ground. He panted and licked his wound.

"What will you do for me if I spare you?" he said.

"Won't do shit for you," she said. "I'll live."

"And do as you please?"

"Damn straight."

The wolf laughed again, hearty and deep this time, then a high-toned laugh that showed all his teeth. He blinked and sniffed the air and looked back at her.

"Fair play," he said. "So long as you never cut your hair, I'll leave you be."

She squinted and touched her head. "I'll do as I please."

The wolf stood, said her name, and sauntered into the woods.

She walked home alone, knife at the ready, wondering who had told the wolf her name.

The blood of the wolf was on her hands, and the stain lingered for days, warming her skin. His coarse fur had stroked her wrist as the knife went in, stroked her neck, her thighs when she dreamed.

The wolf circled her for weeks, teasing her from the edges of clearings, whimpering. Sometimes he even winked at her, with his thick, soft ears standing high. She spit at him and threw her shoulders back so that her hair swooped like a shimmering red curtain.

The wolf whimpered all the more when she did this, but he let her be. Instead, he ate fatherless children, and tore out the hearts of eye-shadowed and rouged girls who cooed at him from the high school bleachers, coaxing him into the shadows under the stands until they realized too late what he wanted.

Not much was done by the sheriff about these lost, devoured girls. Not much ever is.

The following year she fell pregnant and married a doughy, hairless boy who worked for the county.

"Sink your teeth into my neck a little," she told her new husband.

"What on earth," he said. "You're like a wild thing."

"You should grow a beard," she said, but he refused.

He was a good father. She never felt the need to stab him, and right up until the day he died—stringing Christmas lights on the spire of the county courthouse, slipped and fell at age twenty-seven—he never once tried to eat her.

The wolf came again in her thirties. Her children were almost grown, and the youngest of her three daughters had just begun her monthlies. One day while hanging laundry, she saw a patch of auburn fur behind a blooming rhododendron. She patted her hair—so long she had to keep it in a fat bun—then finished putting her daughters' camisoles and bloodstained panties on the line and went inside. All her children were at school. She peeked out from behind her lace curtains and watched as the wolf approached the clothesline to sniff her daughters' garments. He did so for only a moment, then he sat in the grass and stared at the house. Still as stone.

The wolf's black eyes made her hungry.

I see, she thought, feeling a new, delicious ache in her belly. I know what he means now.

When the wolf had gone, she scooped up her keys and her new bone-handled barlow knife and marched to her truck. She rumbled down her steep gravel drive, all the way down, then turned left instead of right and went deeper into the cove, away from town, as deep as the mountain road would take her. When she arrived at a bedraggled stacked-stone house with five rusty Mustangs parked in the weeds, she got out and nodded to Arthur, the big man on the porch.

Arthur dealt in pills and pot and whatever else people needed to get by. Inside he kept six loaded pistols and three prosthetic legs— one for running, one for everyday use, and a shiny titanium one for special occasions.

Arthur raised a slack hand and nodded in return. She walked through the weeds to meet him. Today he had left off his fake leg and sat scratching the stump of his knee in the warm sun.

Arthur called her name as she approached. "Been a while," he said.

"I'm wanting a muzzle," she said. "A good one."

Behind Arthur's house was a maze of dog pens and runs. He was a breeder, and when not selling illicit substances, Arthur dealt in working pups. Malinois, Alsatians, a few hounds. His dogs were cool-tempered and thick-bodied, never mean or half-starved. Unlike most breeders in these parts, he fed his dogs and reared them properly, taught them to hunt and guard and fight without raising hell. What his customers did with these brutes was their business, but while they were here, he liked to say, they were treated like knights.

"A muzzle," he said. "Didn't know you kept a dog."

"I don't. But I got one coming to visit, and I don't trust the owner."

Arthur frowned and leaned forward. "Honey," he said, "why don't you just tell them not to come?"

She flicked her hand to indicate that the situation was complicated.

"Well, I got all kinds. Go on in the kitchen, shelf by the back door, and pick you out one."

She did as instructed, and she came out holding a bright yellow muzzle made of thick straps and steel rings. Arthur refused to charge her.

"Just bring it back when you're done with it," he said, "so I know you didn't get yourself bit."

They had both lived in this cove a long time. When Arthur lost his leg in the war and shipped home to find that his momma had run off and overdosed, she had brought him supper every day for two months.

She thanked him and walked back to the truck.

"Whatever breed it is," Arthur called, "don't turn your back on him."

She leaned out of the open window. "Learned that lesson already," she said, and drove home.

The next morning the wolf came as the girls were piling into the school bus. She saw him appear under a hemlock, back haunches taut, black eyes staring at her middle daughter. His mouth was open and wet.

She stood in front of her daughters and met his gaze. The wolf cocked his head. She raised her hand, palm out, firm. The wolf sat in the leaves and waited.

Once the bus drove off, she walked back up to the house, the whole way hearing the wolf follow her through the brush nearby.

She walked into the house and left the door open. She took the muzzle and her knife from her purse and sat down in her armchair, tucking her weapons out of sight between the cushions.

"Come on, then, old cur," she said, and before she could finish saying it, the wolf pranced right through the door.

The wolf was lithe, more wiry than she'd remembered. Perhaps he had aged, like she had.

"I don't like the way you look at my girls," she said.

The wolf lay on his belly, casually licked a paw. "They favor you. The middle one has your hair."

"You'll not touch them."

"I made a bargain for your life," said the wolf, "not theirs."

"Then we'll just have to make a new bargain," she said. "We'll set new terms."

Her hair was tangled in a tortoiseshell clip. She reached up and let it down. It fell past her shoulders, past her knees, and floated across the arms of the chair.

"I want something from you," she said.

The wolf lowered his head. He knew what she meant. "You want two things from me, then."

She produced the muzzle from under the cushion, and the wolf bared his teeth.

"You don't trust me?"

"I want to be sure of you," she said. "And if you do as I say and wear this in my house, you can have me as long as you like, under one condition."

The wolf's eyes swung from the muzzle, to her hair, to her body, then to her eyes, and back to the muzzle again. "Your daughters," he said.

"You'll not have them, wolf," she replied.

The wolf crawled on his belly toward her. He stayed low down in front of her chair and let her fix the muzzle over his snout. When she had made sure it was secure, she stood and took off her dress, then lay down beside the wolf.

"Agreed," he said, sighing.

And oh, how they took to each other. Scent of pine, hair on fur, spit and sweat and lust, the whole house shaking. They were raw and knowing and beguiled together, and they took delight in each other until neither could breathe without rasping.

As the afternoon lengthened, the wolf became restless, and she announced that the girls would be home soon from school.

"Take this off," said the wolf, scratching at the muzzle with his front paw.

"Go out on the porch," she said. The wolf went outside and stood, waiting. She closed and locked the door behind him and went to the window. She opened it a crack, just enough to get her hand out, and unlatched the muzzle.

"Come again tomorrow," she said, closing the latch and watching the wolf run back into the woods.

The wolf returned the following day, and they repeated everything the same.

"Come again tomorrow," she said, after taking his muzzle off through the window again. That night she giggled herself to sleep and dreamed of his fur brushing her thighs. The wolf visited her every day for a whole season, and each day was the same: low-down he came, then muzzle, fuck, and heaven.

At the close of spring, the wolf disappeared, and she did not see him again for many years. In the papers she read stories of unsolved murders in another county, where the bodies of girls were found heartless, fleshless, buried neatly in the snow. But he kept his word, and her own daughters lived. They lived, and two of them married, and one of them had children—two boys and a sweet girl who called her Meemaw.

March was cold, and the cancer made her shiver worse than she ever had. Her arms ached when she lifted medicine to her lips. She could hear her bones grinding in their sockets. She waited for the wolf.

When he finally came, on a frigid and moonless night, she was momentarily disappointed. His fur had thinned in patches, and he was gray at the snout. His muscles seemed loose under his coat, no longer taut sinew but more like hanging meat. She could see a faint scar where she had stabbed him decades ago.

"Who am I to judge?" said Meemaw, when the wolf saw the way she looked at him.

"I am endangered," said the wolf, raising his chin with pride.

It was true. There were no red wolves left in these parts. Farmers and sheriffs, angry at all the murders in their towns, had shot almost every specimen. The wolf told Meemaw he had no brothers left. In their place, coydogs and invasive, fat coyotes now roamed the woods, tearing open the bellies of newborn calves, stealing soft house cats from their owners. Coyotes had no respect for the mountains they had migrated to, said the wolf. There was no bargaining with them, no finesse.

"No scent of pine, neither," said Meemaw.

"You should lock your door," said the wolf.

"I knew you were coming," she replied.

"But if it had not been me," he said, "what would you have done?"

She nodded at her barlow knife on the table. "Guess I'd have fought off some coyotes."

The wolf sneered at the thought. "Those mongrels would tear you apart." He looked out the window. "They would leave you splayed and naked in your own parlor. They savor no meal."

"Maybe that's all I deserve," said Meemaw. "After all, what am I? Just an old, sick woman nobody sees anymore."

"I see you," said the wolf. "Bright as day. Sweet as milk. Ever so."

"Doctor says I'm all eat up with cancer," said Meemaw. She snorted a bitter little laugh. "What will I taste like?"

"Has the cancer reached your heart?"

"Don't think so," said Meemaw. "Just my titties, and my liver and things. Heart beats fine. They say my blood pressure's still as low as a swimmer's."

"Then that's all that matters," said the wolf, with a slow twitch of his tail. "That's the only bit I want."

Meemaw sighed. The wolf sniffed, then half closed his eyes and sniffed again.

"And your flesh, of course," he said. "I must have that. How I have wanted it, for so long."

Meemaw sighed again. "Do you remember?"

"The first time? At the creek?" said the wolf.

Meemaw nodded. "I was just a young'un. Didn't know a thing," she said, "except that you smelled so good, and I couldn't stand to go near you or I'd faint."

The wolf's lips drew back slowly across his teeth.

"I'd faint from wanting it," she said. "That smell all over me and inside me."

"You smelled of rose water and dill weed," he said.

It was Meemaw's turn to smile. "All those pickles my momma made me put up every summer."

"Ah yes," said the wolf, raising his nose high. "Your mother."

Something in his manner in that moment, in the way he mentioned her mother, brought a new worry to her brain. An awful thought pulsed under her cheekbones and made them grow hot. "You knew my momma?"

The wolf said Meemaw's name, the one her mother had given her, the one no one called her anymore. He said it again. Then he asked, "Don't you know how old I am?"

More awful thoughts filled her brain and began to multiply, to fester, and Meemaw found herself flinching with a strange, newfound fear.

"And the second time," said the wolf, changing the subject. He drew a slow breath, and when he exhaled, she could smell rotting flesh. "The season you outsmarted me with that muzzle."

She tensed her shoulders and pushed her hair behind her ears. "I never did trust you."

"Yes, rightly so." He rubbed his paw on his snout as if remembering the bite of the muzzle's straps. "You were so strong. That was a good spring."

Meemaw had to agree.

"And you were satisfied, and I kept our bargain?"

She agreed again, but warily. "I still hold you to it."

The wolf closed his eyes. "When will you die?"

She stammered a little, then replied, "They give me eight months."

The wolf nodded. "Winter, then," he said.

Outside, a squirrel alighted on the porch railing, twitched its tail, and chittered. The sound reminded Meemaw of a rusted hinge creaking open.

"Wolf?" she said. "I'm frightened."

He nodded again, and his voice was soft. "Then I can take you now, if you wish."

Meemaw looked around her little house, the matching curtains with blue lace, the woodstove, family portraits on the far wall. In the pass-through between her parlor and her kitchen sat a row of prescription bottles, all lined up on the counter. The plastic pill bottles gleamed under the kitchen light like cylinders of amber. She thought of the nausea, of possibly losing her hair, of months of weakness and cost and pain. Her body was tired. As she stared at the pills, the wolf sniffed her and prowled around her chair. Surrendering to him would be better than a slow, wasting death, would it not? The wolf was offering her a kindness. Was that what it was? Could she call it love?

"Tell me something," she said.

"Yes," said the wolf.

"Was I beautiful?"

The wolf said her name once more. He nodded tenderly, then ripped open her throat in one clean, painless bite.

A few hours later, Meemaw's granddaughter pulled up to the house in a battered silver coupe. She got out, arms loaded with two quilts and several plastic containers full of cornbread, and crunched across the gravel to Meemaw's front door.

The lamps inside were off, but the porchlight glowed bright. She looked around, and by the door she saw a strange, shiny mass of some sort of rotten offal. The meat was gray and sickly, and looked as if it had been chewed and spit out.

"Hello?" she called, and knocked on the door. "Meemaw, are you cooking in there? You can't leave trash out here for the animals; you'll get ticks and all kinds of awful things coming in here."

She pushed open the unlatched door. Her long red hair, just like her grandmother's, draped down her back like a cape.

What did she know? Nothing. Poor girl.

The granddaughter went inside and called again. She walked back to the bedroom, and found the wolf in her Meemaw's bed, spent and rapturous, sniffing the old woman's dress.

Teeth white, eyes black. Ears like velvet. The granddaughter trembled. Scent of pine, muscle, and fur.

"You are not one of her daughters," said the wolf.

"N-no," she said. "I'm her granddaughter."

The wolf smiled, slow and lustful. "Indeed," he said.

"What... what should I do?" she asked.

"Do as you please," said the wolf, and the granddaughter fainted.

When she awoke, she was lying on her grandmother's bedroom floor, and the wolf was sniffing her stomach.

"Sweet as milk," he said.

The wolf ate the granddaughter in one gulp, giving no pleasure to her, none of the slow rapture of being devoured and known. He savored her but gave nothing in return. He was a beast, after all, and that is what beasts do. She knew only for a few moments that there was an endangered red wolf who hungered for her, felt only the first flicker of that exquisite terror, and then the next moment she was in his belly.

Once inside him, the granddaughter lit a match and found her grandmother, resting there in the belly of the wolf. Meemaw was curled up in a sleeping position, smiling and dead and torn open. Her granddaughter recognized Meemaw's hair, the silver needles of light in her tresses.

The granddaughter was whole, but she would soon perish in the wolf's gut. She could already feel his muscles pushing against her, and his stomach acid beginning to dissolve her soft skin. Nothing about the experience made her feel beautiful or special, not even for a moment, and she wept for herself, and for the lovely body she had lost.

Meemaw, the girl noticed just before her last match went out, was not whole. Almost all of her grandmother was there, but her breasts were missing, and most of her guts. The wolf had not eaten all of her, not the parts riddled with cancer. The granddaughter remembered the strange mass of tissue on the porch. She shuddered and wept and waited for death.

In the fading matchlight, the girl saw that her grandmother's heart glistened and pulsed atop the heap of womanly, satisfied flesh.

The wolf had eaten Meemaw's heart last.

He had left her tumors for the crows.

COMMON GROUND

by MELISSA SCHRIEK

EL PARAISO

by SALVADOR PLASCENCIA

To STEP ONTO THE field, you needed a player's ID—a piece of cardstock with your name and picture on it. The photograph, which you provided, was coated in a thick, tamperproof film so that even the photo of Caballo, who used mattefying face moisturizers and blotting papers, took on the greasy complexion of the lamination.

In the neighborhood, gardeners and day laborers rented movies and kept beer tabs on the honor of their soccer credentials alone.

I cut a square from a strip of photos I'd had taken at the bus depot. The booth was a holdover from when they used passport two-by-twos for commuter passes. From when the row of pay phones was still there, and girls in frayed shorts chewed gum into the handsets while, on the other end of the line, their boyfriends spoke of turning hulls of rust and Bondo into glinting Chevelles. Once, an abuelita—"Mijo," she said—called me over to help her dial an 800 number followed by a PIN, and then an eleven-digit sequence that would connect her to the Salvation Army's Pasadena Adult Rehabilitation Center. When I tried to hand back the receiver, she said, "Could you please ask for my son, Fulano So-and-So?"

A voice finally came on, tensing the phone line into a garrote. "Who are you?"

That was the era of prepaid phone cards and Chaka. Before data charges. Before art students discovered wheat paste.

The channel 7 anchorman, his pockmarks patched and his hair pomaded into a Pat Riley slickback, had called Chaka the most prolific vandal in Los Angeles history. He narrated over a clip of grainy security footage showing a figure jumping into the transport yard and spray-painting the fleet of buses. The segment segued to an on-scene reporter. The camera panned over the chain-link enclosure and then, finding that the convoy had dispersed, abruptly cut to a shot of the photo booth in the bus depot. Chaka's graffiti hung above the coin slot.

We set the VCRs for the late-night rebroadcast. With our fingers on the REWIND button, we saw the sixteen hundred hours of court-ordered community service to come: Chaka buffed his name from the buses' side panels, picked up the Krylon cans from the floor, and tucked them into a knapsack.

Chaka's name, though not always in his own hand, went on to appear throughout the world. In Nirvana's "Smells Like Teen Spirit" music video, Dave Grohl forged Chaka's tag onto the face of his kick drum. The letters were spaced and scribed in the languid strokes of someone who has yet to be blindsided by a nightstick or flogged by the angry garden hose of a homeowner.

Eventually, a beat cop tackled Chaka as he was writing on a utility pole. What looked like cavitied teeth skittered across the blacktop. They turned out to be only the used spray can nozzles he had stuffed into his pockets. His smile remained intact.

From San Diego to San Francisco, his name was repeated fifty thousand times. On bridges, phone poles, railroad cars, freeway signs, Spanish-style bungalows, ranch houses, county apartments, privately patrolled condos, Neighborhood Watch aluminum placards. The choice of the object or structure constituted the first part of the creative act. Then there were the unseen but implied elements of the work: him scaling cinder block walls, draping cardboard over razor wire, looping his nylon belt into a harness to shuffle up utility posts.

But the significance of the mark was the mark itself. The signified was the signifier. From the Metropolitan State Hospital in Norwalk, his statement to his soon-to-be-prosecutors was simply "Chaka is Chaka."

Back then, to be Mexican and young in the United States meant that you were either the timid child whom housekeepers dragged along as a translator; the muscle-shirted Mario Lopez, who played A. C. Slater on *Saved by the Bell*; or a steering column and screwdriver away from grand theft. The aim, despite Chaka's René Magritte pose, was to overwrite the billboards, the city's surfaces, the hand-painted wood siding, with a relentless work ethic. In doing so, he would interrogate anonymity, celebrity, the destruction necessitated by every aesthetic gesture, and the gaps in commercial and home security systems.

After the newscasts and the flickers of MTV fame, they bolted a panel of Plexiglas to the photo booth to protect the tag from defacement. And, like that, the booth became a monument to a lost era of Chicano art.

In high school, on late nights after standing around sharing a mound of asada fries in an Alberto's parking lot, we'd cross the avenue, go up the depot's stairs, and pass the men who had arrived too early for their Greyhound. From the way they sat on dewed benches and leaned their heads against the walls, they could only be people on the lam. Used to wet seats and scratching their ringworm against stucco. The rope-knotted boxes that accompanied them, gouged by Bic pens, announced their destinies: Calexico. Nogales. El Paso. La Chingada.

On the median where passengers waited for their buses, vending machines dispensed toothpaste, no-rinse soaps, and hard, vacuum-packed cubes that unfurled into unisex Fruit of the Looms. Sometimes a society of paranoids picklocked the cases and tucked pamphlets into the spirals. Along with your new pair of underwear, complimentary literature on the impossibility of the Warren Commission's single-bullet explanation or the addresses and phone numbers of the unquestioned suspects in Kurt Cobain's murder would dispense from the machine.

We spun the booth's stool to its lowest thread, crammed in, and closed its scratchy curtains. Inside, the lesser tags—pudgy letters in paint stick and marker—had been painted over. A single coat of primer obscured the names, but the hues of the ink seeped through to contuse the walls.

Even then, Caballo carried a compact mirror and tweezers. When the sliver of wet paper and chemical reek appeared—the colors washed out and each mug shot bordered by a harsh whiteness—Caballo's thick and perfectly arched eyebrows jutted out of the photographs. And the sequence of squares, like celluloid cells, followed the motion of Santiago nodding his dopey head.

Flipping through the plasticized team deck, you'd see Sears wallet portraits, prints of snaggletoothed grins from orthodontist visits, faces chopped off from group pictures. All our midfielders maimed of cheeks and chins.

Play sloped in favor of the southern goal. Tire tracks bit into the sod. We plucked shards of glass from the dirt. Without linesmen to call offsides or out-of-bounds, a lone referee blew his whistle from the far end of the field. We played under a single age division; teenagers, their gelled fins of hair pointed forward, barreled into old men who smelled of arnica rubs. Three generations of one family bickered over a back pass into the box. Hastily elected goalies slipped borrowed gardening gloves onto their hands and waited under a sagging crossbar. Starters substituted themselves out and, on a prima donna's whim, back into the pitch. Uniforms vaguely matched. Or they matched too closely and duplicate numbers passed the ball to each other. Rorschachs of bleach-stained shirts and shorts.

But there was one hard rule, printed bilingually on the lineup sheets and spray-painted on a flapping tarp that hung from the chain link fence:

NO ID=NO PLAY

SIN CREDENCIAL NO SE JUEGA

We could have gone to a different league. To the West Covina complex, a former landfill covered in Bermuda grass, its turf cut from the same farm that carpeted Dodger Stadium. To the Pasadena clubs that reserved the mowed perimeter around the Rose Bowl. Or to Whittier Narrows, mostly dirt fields but dutifully chalked and stabbed with bright corner flags. But Caballo, Santiago, and I had been in the local liguilla for over a decade, ever since we were cut from the JV squad.

I was staying in my childhood home with my father, but even back when I lived in graduate housing, I rode the bus to our Sunday matches. Caballo never left the neighborhood; if he wanted, he could walk the four blocks to the field. Santiago, down in Irvine, drove in on weekends to check on his mom and then headed back to law school after the games.

A Mickey Mouse league with awful soccer, no doubt, but during my Middle English seminar—this was before the PhD program decided to throw me out—I would drift off and replay the weekend's game. Shanked shots in front of an open net, the brief moments of tiqui-taca. I'd do a complicated calculus to determine what was necessary for our team to reach the knockout stage. In class, we discussed the circle motifs in Thomas Malory's *Le morte d'Arthur*: iron horse hitches, garlands, rings of gold, the doubly circular image of men gathered at the Round Table, the galloping routes going nowhere, the implied halo of Lancelot, the rim of the sangrail. My classmates—imported from what must have been calendar-less towns, who could not orient themselves in time without spotting heaps of unraked leaves, hearing snowplows pushing their salted slush, or picking at the scabbed mosquito bites on their pale legs—nodded at the indisputable presence of the circle.

During breaks and in the hallway, I overheard them calling freeways "interstates," swap meets "flea markets," the West Covina throngs that overtook the Echo Park bars "the bridge-and-tunnel crowd." They marveled at the casual scoops of guacamole that came with their food orders.

Because I had a facility for books, as my mother had told me, I would not be a donkey in the world. But in that room, my skills waned. I did not understand the significance of the patterns. Why had we committed two hours to deliberating the shore of an oblong lake and how it fit the typology of the circular? I felt my skull calcifying. Thickening. It was a small classroom. If I leaned back, the top rail of my chair stopped against the wall. I put the weight on the hind legs of the seat, but instead of the backrest, the back of my head bumped into the plasterboard. It had not been a single motion or an accidental slip. I repeatedly rocked my head into the wall until the professor, a man who lectured into a thick photographic reproduction of the original Malory, a man we knew not by his face but by the sheen of a cyclopean liver spot on the top of his scalp, goofily craned his neck and tried to locate the source of the thumping.

It had been three years since my mother died in her sleep. She'd been so proud, but with her gone, there wasn't much need to continue as a less-than-middling graduate student. She often repeated the name of the school and emphasized that it was private. One day I would be called "doctor," she said.

When her supervisor reached my phone, before telling me what she suspected—that something was wrong—she asked if I was "the son at the university."

"What are you studying?" she said, as if trying to verify what my mother had told her.

She was Korean, but my mother called her La Chinita. The boss who forbade her from sipping water near the cuts of fabric and padlocked the restrooms between breaks.

"Tomasita did not come to work today. She always comes in. Is she okay?" Eventually, I would meet this woman. She would grab my hands and say, "Tomasita was a very hard worker."

During the service, I would feel the residual balm of her vanilla lotion on my fingers, as her sobs cut through the mumbles of prayer.

When you lose your mother, I had read, a levitating pain possesses you. You try to fall onto your bed but find yourself floating in the air space of your room. But the pain I felt was outside of me, as if buried in the dirt. A subterranean and satellite organ. A mangled gland secreting an ache. Some nights I found myself on the floor trying to dig it out.

Saturdays, my mother used to clean houses, but during the week she worked bent over a sewing machine in a Vernon shop. The motor, activated by a step accelerator, spit out long shavings of fabric. Thin cords that ended up in her pockets and clung to her sweater. Scraps I would then see in the kitchen wastebasket.

As a protest against the La Chinita, my mother and her coworkers planned to pee themselves while they diligently hemmed at their workstations. A soft revolt. The kind that could be mistaken for a series of accidents. But when the day came, no one could bring upon themselves the humiliation of wetting their own chairs.

And yet this woman whom my mother had plotted against with her own urine recognized what my father had not. My father had lifted himself from the very mattress my mother lain on, slipped into his maintenance blues, left for work, and never noticed that she had stopped breathing.

When I think of those weeks, it is not an image of my prone mother and her yellowed soles and heels that comes to mind. Instead, I remember the elegantly dressed Korean woman—a funeral kimono, people said—walking down the church's side aisle. A collective flinch of deference parting the way for her.

*　*　*

Soccer is a form of forgetfulness. Your mother, facedown on sheets sewn from three swaths of cloth. The stack of theory your professors saddled you with: xeroxes of corroded and speckled sentences instructing you in how to read a novel. The fact that the world buys the trifold wallets of Shepard Fairey—a RISD-trained plagiarizer, offspring of a doctor and a Realtor, and owner of a Sunset gallery—and meanwhile Chaka lives in a Bakersfield flophouse. Your father's beard clippings in the kitchen sink. The sulking but aimless lovesickness you feel. All those things that vex you—petty and of the marrow—vanish in the singular task of chasing a ball.

I handed my player ID to the referee—a man leathered by the sun and lumpily muscled from what could only be a lifetime of shoveling gravel into a cement mixer. He inspected the card and then raised his head.

They called me Ray, sometimes Charles, occasionally Bizco. I was not blind or cross-eyed, but it was true that I did not meet people's gaze. Even in pictures, I looked away and to the side of the camera's flash. All those quarters that we fed into the Chaka booth and not once did the lens catch me looking directly at it. It was a paternal disorder aggravated by the amount of time I spent hunched over books. I shared a house with my father and had spent my childhood on my grandfather's farm, but I could not tell you the color of their eyes. Their faces, if I was to describe them: scruff, a splotch of skin, a ridge of cartilage.

"Your last name?" the referee asked to confirm against the card.

"Plascencia," I said.

"Are you from Yahualica?" he asked. Some of the teams were just reconstituted pueblo clubs. Perhaps he thought me a defector from some crumbling adobe he used to pass on his moped.

"No," I said. "I mean, my dad was from there. More Cuquío than Yahualica. A little ranch called Los Sapos."

"I know it," he said. "It's a beautiful valley."

*   *   *

The match turned into a fiasco. An early goal slumped our morale and slackened the formation. We took delusional shots from outside the box, overtired our forwards with long balls, and clumped in ways that left too many easy lanes open. The score, which they then posted on El Paraiso's corkboard, took our goal differential into the cellar.

El Paraiso, a sunken bar with an awning aimed at the heads of the tall and stilettoed, served bottled beers and a single tap of a skunky lager. Food simmered in a vat covered by a wheezing bath towel. In the pot: a rotation of pozole, meat in its juices, chicken mole, and—to irritate one particular faction—the regional sin of hominy and pork in the menudo. Doña Letty, the proprietor and one of those women who towered over whomever was in the room, ladled broth and chunks of meat into chipped clay bowls.

A keloid ridge, like the cartoon scar of that one Crimson Twin, protruded from Doña Letty's temple. The mark of where she had collided with her own awning.

Like at any other bar, promotional neon signs radiated their dusty glow, and posters of bikini models holding cans to their navels plastered the ceilings. A loose theme of Mexican fútbol clubs, beer brands, and cardboard cutouts of smiling women. But then you noticed the wall dedicated to Santa Anita race jockeys. Crop whips extended out of their hands. In some pictures, they stood next to children for additional scale. Behind the squat bar, an autographed jersey of Muggsy Bogues hung over the register.

Framed stills of Jorge Campos in his clownishly tasseled uniforms tiled the hallway leading to the smoking patio. European commentators and scouts said Campos was too short for a goalie. They were mostly right. He stopped direct shots with histrionic leaps, but the soft lobs, despite his spasms to reach and stretch, sailed gently over his head and into the net.

Sundays, our league took over El Paraiso. We'd cross the street, clacking our cleats against the asphalt, and then prop open the door with our bags to air out the room. The unspoken and unenforced rule was that you could not drink before a match. But the late-afternoon games, those preceded by opposing sides coming out of El Paraiso's door together, sometimes devolved into sloppy brawls.

Inside the bar, sweat evaporated and halos of salt crusted our jerseys. Clods broke from our soles into piles of dirt. Scrunched-up socks and shin guards ended up on the tabletops. All other days of the week, Doña Letty ran the place as a fichera bar. She sopped the floors with floral-scented Fabuloso and brought in crops of Baja girls on shopping visas.

Freshly showered construction workers in Stetsons paid a surcharge to sit with a waitress while she brushed her calico wig. The women listened to the men reminisce about their little pueblos and how they would one day return in a double-cabbed Dodge Ram. The bed of the truck would be lined by one of those protective plastic kits and loaded with a generator, bags of soccer balls and uniforms, a crate of peanut butter, nested sets of Teflon pots, vinyl shower curtains, and boxes of neatly folded Marshalls and Ross clothes. From the crest of the hill, where the asphalt roads leading to their pueblo break into dirt, they would spot the frays of smoke from the fogones, and hear the braying donkeys as they downshifted the transmission.

Today, though, the bar was ours. After the match, I sat across from Caballo. He had a fantastic first touch and a huge bubble butt that naturally held off defenders, but he also tended to overheat. His nostrils swelled, and a sheen of sweat slowed him to a trot. If we were without a bench, he'd play full time, halfheartedly walking down to defend and sticking his ass into the passing lanes.

He was also a person who did not take indirect paths to a subject.

"Ray, you played like shit," he said. "And I don't know what you did, but you really fucked it up with my sister."

Cheli was Caballo's sister. Some months before, after a house party where we sat on a kitchen counter, I had ended up in her Honda's backseat. A police officer, one who would later be kicked off the force for shoplifting a hairbrush and a bottle of nail polish remover, flashed a Maglite through the rear window. We looked up at the shine, at the wings of the cop's Siouxsie Sioux eyeliner, and got out of the car. The cop—whom Cheli knew from her high school track days—motioned with her flashlight for us to get in the front seat. She didn't say a word but I understood what she was telling me: *This girl, my old teammate, who is too beautiful and tall for you, deserves more than to have your hand trapped in her underwire on the side of a busy thoroughfare.*

Cheli slowly accelerated past the patrol car. A lone clipboard rested on its passenger seat. The cop was named Stephanie, Cheli told me, after all the white girls her mother imagined she would go to school with. In the locker room, she was all tits and no butt. One generation in—too many Flamin Hots and Cup Noodles—and she already had one of those Chicana bodies that collect all the salt up top.

Cheli drove me to her house. Caballo sat on the porch whittling at a branch like a campesino killing time on the hacienda. She pulled me past him, around one of those thorny bushes planted under windows, and into her garage.

I had never been dragged by the hand in that way. I ended up in women's beds only by the grace of their acquiescence. By their boredom, their pity, their lazy loneliness. Cheli did not act like she was reducing herself for me. She did not wistfully talk about a Colorado poets' colony or ask if I had an ecstasy pill I could split with a box-cutter.

I fell mostly for mousy girls, girls who barely filled their clothes, who believed in the mineral properties of crystals, and who called their parents once a year to announce they would be stopping by for a camping stove and sleeping mats. In other words, women who had matriculated into PhD programs in Poetics and Literature. And then there was Cheli, who frayed every pant pocket, gave half of her paycheck to her mom, and snored next to me under the screen-printed blessing and lowered eyes of the Virgin of Guadalupe.

In the morning, the roosters' territorial crowing woke us. Her father would be pulling in from his graveyard shift soon.

"You should go, but I hope to see you soon," she said. There was nothing to decode in her words.

Absentmindedly, I put my hand on her shoulder and ran it down her arm, rubbing my fingers over the texture of her inoculation scar.

"Don't do that," she said.

In support of El Paraiso's theme, we made fun of Peter Crouch—an English footballer who ran as if on stilts and headed the ball like a giraffe. We complained about the vagaries of our league: the increase in ref fees, the required sportsmanship class you had to attend if you were tossed from a game, the noise of the passing Metrolink train drowning out the offside whistles.

We repeated stories we had already told. I had been dismissed from graduate school and still had to find a job. Santiago spent the week gently studying law, making flash cards for Civil Procedure and Torts. He had sent his brother, Guille, to Guatemala to sober up and to keep him away from a pack of flannelled bald heads.

It was one of those sibling mysteries. How was Santiago—who wore his retainer in broad daylight, kept a change of a button-up shirt and slacks in his soccer bag, and reserved a study carrel on a windowless corner of UC Irvine's library—Guille's Irish twin? In the past, we had joked that Guille would be Santiago's in-house defendant, but it never got that far. On the outskirts of Villa Nueva—in a tiny farming town painted white and red by Marlboro ads—a storm swell had dragged his brother across a bed of rocks.

"I don't think he'd ever seen a river before. The current took him. My 'ama can at least say that. If he'd stayed here, someone was going punch a crowbar through his rotted skull," Santiago said, his corrected overbite shining between his lips.

As for Caballo, he was still the only known straight man managing a Sephora counter.

The league was taking up a collection for Nightcrawler, a notorious time-waster who was always calling for a rounder ball, asking the ref for distance on every spot kick, and writhing on the floor after glancing contact. He had been deported.

While tending goal, he dressed in all-black rash guards, materialized in midair to cradle the ball, and was of that dark complexion that read as blue. It seemed like a waste to hire him a pollero when he could just poof himself across the border. The donations, gathered in a yellowed and ragged tejana, would be moneygramed to him.

In the meantime, Nightcrawler waited in his childhood rancho. A place with a single well, the water pulled up by rope and bucket. Its fallow farmlands overtaken by demon bushes. When people lived there, they'd empty their chamber pots on the side of the main road. Utility poles had been hoisted up, but the town never gathered the bribe for the transformers and the spools of wire. Now corrugated sheets slipped from the roofs of weathered adobes. The only residents, a clump of old men at a dominoes table, gambled away and then hesitantly recouped their plots of parched soil. A place with a forgotten name but marked by its pointless pylons.

By virtue of my birth, I, too, was from a small Mexican rancho. A place called Los Sapos. Its river flowed year-round. Quelites, mushrooms, tender nopal paddles, and red prickly pears sprouted wildly from the ground. Beds of purslane flanked the arroyo at its banks. Purple leafstalks announced their camotillo roots. Rabbits and dinner doves flashed through the foliage.

Men wearing Zapata sombreros, exaggerated brims with tricolor bands, carefully removed rocks they had placed over the wild agave.

The weight of the river stones was used to fold the leaves onto themselves. At the center of the maguey, where the heart of the plant had been gouged at, sap pooled and fermented. They set their hats on the ground and kneeled to slurp, their faces sticky with pulque. Stubbles of gnats gathered at their chins.

Even men like these, my grandfather said, drunkards who spent their days licking cacti and plucking toadstools, could forage a plate of greens and potatoes and roast game meat from their thin snares of twine. Mesquites drooped their sweet pods, and panelita plants bloomed custard buds. And yet my father had abandoned Los Sapos for El Norte, to work as a peon greasing hinges and serrated cogs. To eat leathery thaws of meat and stale bread from plastic bags and drink water thinned by bleach and tanged by rusted plumbing.

In Los Sapos, barely lift a finger and the land gave you plenty. But if you did want to work the furrows, each cornstalk yielded not one but two ears, beans burst their hulls, the hillside flared yellow with squash flowers.

As was the curse, the men outlived the women in my family. But when my grandmother was still alive, she would dump the ash from her fogón at the edge of the maize field. Inside the kitchen, she removed the covering from the freshly cut maize. The husks were flattened and stacked for wrapping gorditas and tamales. The corn silk, little blond nests, she shoved into the mouth of a glass bottle to steep into a tincture.

She would hold an ear of corn in one hand and point at the puny but somehow bloated kernels sprouting from the nose. "When you plant your crop," she said, "unless you want a harvest of sickly maize ears that taste like moldered cow hooves, do not put these in the soil."

When school let out in June, instead of to camps and summer classes, my parents sent me away to Los Sapos. On afternoons when my grandfather was not away pulling barbed wire taut in some field, he parked his Massey Ferguson just outside the house and ran the TV cord through the window's grille. Instead of ending in a pronged plug, the wire split into clamps that clasped onto the tractor's battery posts. Mexico had been knocked out on penalties, so we watched · Argentina's Maradona, the pudgiest and shortest player in the Cup, run past the back lines of Europe. Slashing past England, Belgium, and, finally, West Germany's towering fullbacks. During halftimes, to keep the battery from draining, my grandfather turned on the tractor. As the engine ran and commercials for Fabuloso and Honda mopeds cycled across the screen, my grandfather would bring up my father. My father could have been a rich man on his own land. What kind of foolishness was it to abandon a place like Los Sapos to go live in an apartment with shoddy walls, where you could hear the people next door spitting phlegm, and their turds sluicing down the pipes? my grandfather would say.

It is true, American partitions are a hollow gypsum, but in California, we lived in a stand-alone house. And our neighbors, a Chinese couple who owned the only pizzeria in town, practiced a diligent silence. They drove off to work before dawn and returned only to sleep. I did not correct my grandfather. If they had ever made a noise, I would have remembered.

Those times aside, when we sat on a bench fitted with cushions, and the noise and fumes of the idling Massey Ferguson cut into the World Cup telecast, I remember my grandfather mostly for the things he left in the hallway: a bloodied sickle blade, its teeth blunted and its hilt bare; a skinned snake in a bucket of brine; a cheese basket, its weaving distended by the weight of shell casings soldered to menacing silver tips.

They were not nightmares—I was awake—but while sitting in the kitchen eating the freshly puffed tortillas my grandma pulled from the comal or wading in the river picking up the tiny turtles that sunned on the rocks, these items produced a shiver in my thoughts.

The bullets were for a revolver he stuffed into his pocket and used to spook coyotes and skunks from the coop. The snake, raised on a pole and pointed at the sun's hot spots, would stiffen into jerky.

The red, syrupy discharge on the sickle's serrated edge: the ooze of a fungus that was rotting maize stalks in a boggy vein of tepetate.

What seemed like witchcraft or the aftermath of a violent encounter turned out to be just farmwork. The bloodstains on the shirt he hung on the clothesline, which darkened into a scabbing tint, were but the broken-down sugars of a blighted plant saturated into the polyester blend.

The final time that I saw my grandfather was when we buried my grandmother. A Juchitlán priest with a bowl cut, an indigeno who spoke only Nahuatl and the liturgical language of his seminary, led the service. A member of the order of Juan Diego Cuauhtlatoatzin. We knelt and stood by following his hand motions, but, unable to decode the prompting versicles, we remained silent throughout the ceremony.

I heard my grandfather grumble, as if spitting out a sprig of epazote, "An Indio speaking Latin."

My father and grandfather both wore dark glasses and refused to weep. Their faces swelled. Ballooning until they walked in a bowed posture. Four peons—men hired from town, wearing brand-new dress shoes and holding fresh cuts of synthetic rope scorched at the ends—lowered the coffin.

Husband, son, and grandchild aside, every person at her requiem received a donation or wage.

The night before, my father and I had stayed in a hotel in Cuquío, a town with a police station and a central square, ten miles from Los Sapos. The maids set up their washboards and tubs of bedding in the courtyard. To reach our room, we had to step through gray, sudsy water. Once inside, a scorpion loitered in the shower stall. Rather than stay in Los Sapos, my father preferred to splash in scummy runoff and soap himself over the sink. After the funeral, that same day, we made our way back to Cuquío and to the bus station that would take us back to the city and airport. In a covered remolque, a motorized wagon with a rickety suspension, we sat with the men who had helped carry the casket and shovel the dirt. They had taken off their dress shoes and slipped on their huaraches. Their leathered and fungused toes poked out of their sandals. The sashes of new rope hung across their chests.

Two or ten years after, I could not tell you, news of my grandfather's death arrived in one of those candy-striped envelopes, its postage canceled by penned initials and again by an automated stamp. By deed or next of kin, all of the land—sembradillos of agave, corn, and feed that stretched from the foothills of Los Sapos through the valley—belonged to my father.

By that time, I had already begun to suspect that I was not cut out for literary studies. One of my professors—Porfidio Echeveria, the only professor with a Spanish surname to pass through the eye of the needle into tenure—stood at the podium and read from *The Little Trilogy*. He described the alchemic process of the words traveling as sound waves, softening the earwax of our canals, and then reaching the coil in our skulls. That thing that we felt, the sudden realization of our mortality and stunted passions, the lifting of the emotional grogginess, was Chekhov's words transmuted into iron nano-hammers tapping at our jaded minds.

But I heard only a trill from Echeveria. In Los Sapos, before the sun set, I would walk up the hills, cut across a field of just-transplanted agave—the leaves pale and the thorns still fleshy—and then squeeze between the lines of the barbed wire. My job, as was the job of every child in Los Sapos and the reason our soccer games broke up, was to herd the calves away from their mothers and walk them into a pen before dark.

Sometimes I would come upon a feeding calf. Instead of obediently taking the lead, it would bite into its mother's teats, ram its head and tiny horns into her underbelly, and gag on its own milk. I would throw clods of dirt and dried donkey dung to break them apart and then shepherd the calf down the slope, around the fenced furrows, and into a stone corral. Cut demon bushes—thorny shrubs that I dragged into place—sealed the calf in.

It was not a fully formed hope—at that time I was probably still holding a childhood fantasy of one day playing in Camp Nou and agonizing about what national team I would represent—but I had an inkling of myself as an adult waking in the mornings to the braying cows that had come down to claim their young, tying their hind legs, and filling buckets of milk. I would pour a packet of powdered chocolate into a clay mug and squirt in milk straight from the udders, to make foaming cocoa. After undoing the knot and pulling away a demon bush, mother and young would make their way back up the hill.

Echeveria, a writer whose obscurity was often profiled in week-lies and on public radio, once spoke in aphorisms and direct edicts. Borges was a genius but grew too dependent on the motif of the mirror. Adverbs, like those shriveled vestigial organs inside us, would serve us better if they atrophied out of use. But Echeveria had recently jumped theoretical camps: once a fervent defender of clarity and Spartan declarative sentences, he now believed in the unity of the circular and the fated cyclicity suggested by winding geometries, in the ambiguity of language, in the ephemeral value of any singular interpretation. I was not the most attentive student, so I was not always able to follow. But the turn seemed one of expedi-ency. Before, when he spoke of Chekhov, he had seemed to actually mean what he said.

My classmates, even some that I admired and lusted for, stayed after his lectures to draw circles on the board.

My father never showed any interest in the ranch—I could have quit grad school, taken it over, and run an organic farm. Grown heir-loom corn and beans and packaged them in paper sacks and twine for boutique health food stores. In order to not defraud the name of Champagne, Champagne has to be from its namesake region. By Mexican law, tequila has to be distilled in Jalisco, and I had just come into sixteen acres of Jaliscan blue agave. In time, I could have learned to make my own tequila. My work would have been real. The type that produced from the land and satiated hunger and thirst.

I also, of course, imagined there would be someone with me. I would sit with her as thunderstorms pulsed against the thickly caulked panes of glass. For her, we would need a phone line. Wire would need to be extended from Cuquío, one long furrow fitted with PVC pipes and then covered and packed down in its own dirt. The ring of incoming calls. A number for her friends and editors, a modem for the transmission of her magazine submissions.

But my father, as if donating a patio chair to the Salvation Army, unceremoniously gifted everything away. And that life, far from the toil of literary studies, suddenly passed me by.

One Sunday, back when I was still technically a student, drunk and carrying my soccer bag after a game, I made a pit stop at my father's. I opened the refrigerator: a box of eggs and a two-liter bottle of orange Fanta. In the shower, the shampoo bottle felt full, but it had been filled with water to stretch its dregs. My father was not in the house. If he had been, I told myself, I would ask him why he had given Los Sapos away.

As I locked up the house to head back to campus, a Chevy—one of those rattling pickup trucks with its tags pasted to the wind-shield—backed in and dumped a wooden crate onto the driveway. Clumps of burned clouds shot out of the muffler as it pulled away.

The box, sealed solely by the weight of its lid, contained only one thing: a cache of beige work clothes. The left pocket of every pair of pants had been rubbed down to polyester mesh. At the bottom of the crate, I found what amounted to a handful of petrified animal crackers.

*   *   *

Her name was Molly. It was her I imagined reading Marjorie Perloff and writing poetry—the one who would dial up her manuscripts while I drove the Massey Ferguson and dislodged mud from the tractor's hitch. She grew up in a Chicago suburb. Her next-door neighbor lived in a Frank Lloyd Wright, and Molly had always felt the inadequacy of residing in a house designed by an unknown architect. Molly's area of study focused on nonlinear materialities—an emerging field pioneered by Echeveria. Molly planned to write her dissertation on the subject and, if the university formatting guidelines would allow, submit her work in what she called a "corrective codex" to the library archives.

That novels ended on the last page of the book—she argued— was an arbitrary product of the architecture they were housed in. She gifted me a few of her preliminary codices: chapbooks that unfolded into Möbius strips; a book of paper leaves crudely glued to a cardboard cylinder, resembling a homemade carburetor filter; monographs bound by rings. All unpaginated and ranting about the privileged positions of prologues and the patient deference of codas, an essentialist sequential order that permeated the culture. She repeated these laments in late-night calls from a Denver colony—a colony I sometimes suspected was in reality just the one-room cabin of a boyfriend.

A few weeks after the house party, Cheli and I sat together at a coffee shop table. By then, we had already sat through two different cineplex features. A remake of *Giovanni's Room* set on the Wyoming range, and a darkly lit slasher. She had just finished a double shift. She sipped a red-eye while explaining the complicated hierarchy of nurses. Her rank placed her between those of condescending superiors and a gaggle of trainees who could not fasten a diaper.

"And you're studying English?" she asked.

"I was."

"Like to be a high school teacher?"

How do you defend the urgency of poststructuralism—the greasiness of everything we say—and the nascent field of circular studies to someone who untangles oxygen tubes from the no-longer-breathing and wipes the last dribbles of life force from their chins?

What do the politics of literary taste matter? Cheli, it used to be that I could describe the thick gauge of your hair in my mouth, bite into your neck until I welted you. Feel at you as I reached between your skin and elastic. What resulted did not need to be connected to the erotics of the Ouroboros. But to do that now—to speak straightforwardly—only perpetuates a brute, Neanderthal linearity. That is my understanding of the state of literature, and likely why I flunked exams and professors hesitated to call on me.

"No, not high school, but it doesn't matter, because they kicked me out. I was not the best student, but it was also political."

The story I told her, a bit abridged and without the direct references to Sir Thomas Malory, is as follows.

I was one of the graduate assistants of Porfidio Echeveria, a little-known but exceedingly productive critic. After a long but mostly unheralded publishing history, he found that his star was slowly being pulleyed up by his foray into and conversion to a new compositional approach. Instead of writing on flat surfaces—pieces of paper with clearly delineated (and prejudicial) beginnings and ends—he began to compose his work on candles. As a medium that quickly doubled back on itself, it naturally produced an ambiguity of order in the texts. The publications—all journals of prestige with circulations in the hundreds of thousands—published transcriptions of his work accompanied by photographs of candles turned on their sides.

My job was to do his menial academic work. Xerox, fetch library books, and grade his undergraduates' midterms. Along with the code to the photocopy machine, he gave me duplicates of his office keys. I had passingly, the way I would talk to a janitor or some person at a bar wearing a Pachuca jersey, offered some nicety, but he gave no reply.

I don't even remember the specific thing that I said. There can be misunderstandings. The way Spaniards constantly say filthy things, but it is perfectly civil talk back on their peninsula. Who knew what my Spanish meant outside of the backwaters of Los Sapos? My other suspicion was that he did not know Spanish, so he could not, naturally, respond to what I had said. From that moment on, I always felt a tension in our interactions. He looked at me with distrust, and I, in turn, grew even more suspicious of him.

One evening, after the *MA* seminar—*MA* is what we took to calling *Le morte d'Arthur*—I entered Echeveria's office to pick up a stack of student papers from his desk. The *MA* professor had spent the whole class trying to distance himself from a sentence in an old paper of his that one of the graduate students had unearthed in a database. The professor had written, "Temporal and casual linearity plays a crucial role in *Le morte d'Arthur*; Arthur's life history functions as a framing device, providing a beginning and a clear denouement."

His scalp reddened, and then, as if he had prepared for this incriminating eventuality, he noted that his position had evolved, but even within the argument of the quoted paper, his methodology sought to bend the rigid vectors by emphasizing the coils straining the narrative line.

After tucking the student essays into my bag, I noticed the half-inscribed candle on Echeveria's desk and a printout of his manuscript that he was copying the text from.

It was not Echeveria's radical reenvisioning of writing technologies and practices that had produced his vaunted new prose. He composed the writing in the way he always had—working methodically and linearly from an outline. The scratches on the Pottery Barn candles had transformed an academic life of proposal submissions— proposals that landed Echeveria on early morning panels where his fellow presenters outnumbered the audience members—into one filled with invitations to deliver keynotes in hotel ballrooms. A symposium on Echeveria was in the works. The school was not in a position for another scandal: The university had recently returned a Heisman statuette. Crushed top hats, rinds of watermelon, and washcloths crusted in shoe polish had spilled out of a fraternity's trash bin. A physician from the student health center had left a hard drive behind at a coffee shop; it contained only his name and footage of coeds holding their breasts and then dropping their hands at his medical urging. The files were meticulously organized by hair color.

I acted as if I were unaware of what I was saying—by the water fountain, in the TA lounge, walking up the two flights of steps that led to the department, as my classmates discussed the sauce on In-N-Out Burgers. I simply described what I had observed in Echeveria's office. Eventually, word got to the department chair and she called me in.

I had flunked the departmental exam. I did not know the name of the narrator of Ellison's *Invisible Man*. I could not accurately summarize the plot of *Nightwood*. In my traversal of Pavić's *Dictionary of the Khazars*, I took the least sophisticated of paths. They would need me to leave. But despite these shortcomings, the department chair offered me a master's degree as severance. Also, she said, Echeveria— in this theoretical and material work—had revolutionized the field and elevated the prestige of the entire department. What great thinker had not been maligned and slandered by some disgruntled graduate student?

I told Molly, whom I was seeing at the time, that Echeveria was a fraud, and that I was thinking about writing a letter to the MLA.

"That would be the Lee Harvey Oswald way of making a name," she said.

"But what does it matter how he wrote it if he wrote it?" was Cheli's response. Just outside the coffee shop's window, an order of

Juan Diego Cuauhtlatoatzin—an image of the Virgin of Guadalupe silkscreened onto their scapular coverings—passed in procession. The coxswain, I gathered, shouted directions to turn right and hold the line at the corner. On Tepeyac Hill, Juan Diego spoke in Nahuatl to the Virgin Mother, but to order their procession to yield at a traffic light and then look both ways, it was in Latin that the monks now shouted.

"I love those monks," Cheli said. "They just walk around all day, picking wrappers and beer cans off the ground and looking for old ladies to help across the street."

As she said this, a sarcastic, vulgar phrase manifested itself in my thoughts: *Indios speaking Latin.* Sometimes we cannot escape the gross parlance of our grandfathers.

"I want to show you something," she said and pulled up the sleeve of her maroon nurse's scrubs.

She had tattooed over her vaccine scar. They had shaved off a patch of arm hair and placed an oily, puffy swirl on her dark and furred arm.

"Archimedes's spiral?" I asked.

"What's that?"

"Nothing. Never mind."

"How can it be nothing?"

"It doesn't matter."

"Are you being an asshole, Ray?"

Of course, that was not my name, but we had met through the juvenile idiocy of soccer. She had come to watch her brother play and overheard grown men call at me for the ball. I had never corrected her.

"It's not?" she said.

"Like your brother's name is not really Caballo."

"But that's obvious. No one is going to name their kid Horse. All this time, and I don't even know your real name? There is something really fucked-up about you. Like those schools you went to fucked with your head."

Freckles lit her face and fell into her mouth and down her neck.

But then one of her eyelashes came unhinged. I saw the smudges of foundation rubbed into her blackheads and the cheap metal of her studs swelling her earlobes.

After my mother's funeral, I walked home with my father. The church was two blocks from the depot, and buses and cars bunched up at the red light as we crossed the street. A Mercedes stopped just over the pedestrian stripe. Through the windshield, I saw her. My mother's boss, I thought, but then quickly corrected myself. It was not her. I felt a slight wincing of my conscience. Whatever the Germans call that sensation when you confuse one person for another, that private and faint shame that overtakes your thoughts for trying to make one person into another.

But instead of searching my mind for the word, I tried to fill the quiet. We were wearing the same funeral clothes, new but the same, that we had last worn in Los Sapos. As we passed the bus station, I told my father the story of Chaka and the photo booth. How Chaka was the only artist to convert the whole of California into a ready-made art object. But now Chaka, carrying on under his legal name—Gonzalez, Ramos, Lopez: I could not remember—lived as an émigré in a Bakersfield hotel room over a liquor store. One of those shops with warped plywood for windows and MILLIONAIRE MADE HERE banners drooping from the eaves. The most important Chicano writer of the past twenty years, even more so than Arturo Islas and Anzaldúa, and none of my professors had heard of him. He nodded as if he understood the sadness of what I had said.

We passed a group of men squatting in a circle and blowing into a mound of embers. What they had done, my father explained, was drop kernels into a hole and then pack it with cow pats. They would spend all night blowing at the dung and picking the popped corn from the dirt and ashes. From the way he described the process, in detail and tenderly, I thought he was going to tell me a story about my mother. How he had first spotted her while puffing into a fire. Or, maybe, that he would ruminate on the importance of the seeds—the spiritual and caloric sustenance of the Mesoamerican people. How even if we accounted for the mestizaje of the conquest, we were people bound to the land.

"Some people come to the United States and still eat the same cow shit and offals they ate when they lived in dirt towns" was how he concluded.

I was slurping my pozole and working the meat from the pig's foot. Santiago had gone home to read appellate briefs. Caballo piled cabbage and radishes onto his plate. I was thinking of Cheli; I was. But Molly had called the night before and left a message, and she kept crossing my mind. She had not spoken into the phone but instead played a loop of sound by an experimental poet. I had downloaded the message and listened to it again and again, tried to untangle its meaning. That was the problem, she would say: I took an intricate brooch and pounded it out into a line of wire.

"I'm not rubbing it in, but I want you to know, la cagaste," Caballo said. Sweat had coagulated his designer eyebrow gel into nits of lard. "Cheli's going out with that cop now. I know she's not a cop anymore, but she still wears the jacket. Shows up with her Rite Aid concealer and crumbling highlighter pencil around her eyes. Knocks on our door all shameless and then heads to the garage."

Two tables over, the referees counted bills out of the collection hat. It was not quite enough to bring Nightcrawler back, but another pass in a week might do the trick. The referee with the Popeyed arms, veined and rubbed bare, grabbed his beer bottle and took two tottering steps toward us. Gingerly, he maneuvered into a chair.

He was drunk, but instead of slurring his words, he slowed to articulate each syllable. "Plascencia, right?"

I nodded. He set his elbows on the table. He had a story to tell me, he said.

"Your grandfather was a man they called El Zarco. He carried animal crackers in his pants pocket—cheap cookies from a ten-pound sack. Elephants and camels maimed of their trunks and humps, which he offered from his uncalloused white palm. With his other hand, maybe his left one—whatever hand Cain used to stone his brother— he shot at us. He killed my neighbor, my grandfather, and one of my great uncles. He carried a cob revolver— a pistol that sounded like a larded pot of bursting kernels—and shot at them until they fell."

The referee retracted his arms and took a sip from his empty beer can and then, calmly, went on to explain.

During the war, the Cristeros— church people—set fire to the government offices and registries. Much, much later, the government decided to reissue all those land deeds. My grandfather went around collecting those pieces of paper, sticking his gun into people's windows.

"He had blue eyes, and the law was a full day's walk from Los Sapos. The Juchitláns he left alone; he had no language with which to threaten them, and they had no papers to surrender.

"No one ever even threw a rock at his house, but he died a lonely man. He was buried, but it was only to keep his stench from the air."

As the referee said this, he searched for my eyes. When I finally gave in to his stare, I felt a deep shame jolt through my bloodline.

I was a short man in America and the progeny of a murder. I was without a vocation. I did not know which way to direct my love or penitence. I lived among people haunted by the ghosts of tiny pueblos.

Whether literature was cyclical or an unbending arrow, I no longer believed in it. Sentences, those inert marks, had bent me into a hunchback and kept me from looking up. As a doctoral student, I received a regular paycheck, subsidized housing, two weekly meals at the dining hall, a pair of prescription glasses, and an annual dental cleaning, concluding with a parting bag of floss and a firm-bristled toothbrush. All of these things I received, and all I had to do was read. My earlier gratitude for this fact now seemed like one of those stupid acts of politeness—like thanking a traffic cop after being handed a ticket, or bowing appreciatively as your shoes and shirt deny you entry into a restaurant.

I did not know if I wanted to call Cheli. Or what to think of my father. Or if I would now have to leave the league.

So I drank with Caballo. Told him that I missed his sister, but sometimes this white girl from school would get stuck in my skull.

"That's meningitis, Ray. If it doesn't feel like a kidney shot or it hurts in the liver, then it's not real." He was botching Oscar De La Hoya into Chavela Vargas.

We sat there with our stupid talk until the keg spit out its airy foam and we were the only ones left in El Paraiso. A barrel-bellied man poked his head in. Mother-of-pearl and silver shone from his buttons and belt buckle. He eyed the stretch of the room expectantly and then lowered his cowboy hat to his chest in confusion. Nightcrawler's soccer ID, an unpaid tab paper-clipped behind it, hung from a clasp behind the counter. Doña Letty told the man to come back in a day, and then, ducking to avoid the overhead lamps of her own bar, made her way toward us.

Onto a tray she slid our bowls of pork bones, empty pint glasses, and the bottle the referee had left behind.

"Time to head out, chapos," she said. With a perfumed dishrag, she wiped away our greasy handprints and the tiny but visible dander we had molted as we sat there. Rubbing the cloth into the grain until a sheen returned to the tabletop.

DREAMERS

by Christina Wood Martinez

DREAMS, ISAAC'S MOTHER TOLD him, are a private matter. Like genitals or one's room, they are meant to be looked after and made use of in whatever manner their owner thinks best. Isaac had dreams, many that he enjoyed very much—invisible bicycles and dinosaurs you could saddle and ride—and some of which served as inspiration for schoolyard scenes and schemes. Some he didn't care for at all. Rambling quests with ungraspable missions. Arguments. Lost trails. These were the dreams that went on endlessly. You forgot you could do anything but dream them, so unlike the ones that woke you, swift snap, as when his father took a hold of his ankles and pulled him across the lawn, down the black bore of the sewage drain.

Tonight, he was standing in a narrow hole, surrounded by snow, looking up at a sky nearly as white. Had he fallen through a snowdrift? He wasn't sure. He stood for a long time, arms pinned. No way out. No one to call to. Not waiting, not afraid. This pocket of snow was where he was and would be. He wore a coat but it wasn't all that cold.

That was the whole of the dream. He woke and it was still deep night. How could a mind come up with all that bright white in a room so dark? He felt shamed by the dream. Only after waking did it seem frightening, how easily he had surrendered. He could have gone to his mother's room and told her he'd had a nightmare, but he didn't like it when she comforted him. He fixed his thoughts on a happy thing: there had been a dog at a school assembly that week. A golden Lab that knew its multiplication tables. When its trainer asked it to multiply two and two, it barked four times.

NO TEARS IN THE TYPING POOL was what the sign said. It wasn't library policy. Sigrid, distraught about something, had handwritten the sign more than a year ago and taped it to the back of the door, a kind of slogan for the transcriptionists, though Katherine had never shed tears while typing nor seen either of the other two cry. Their job, typing the text of audio recordings and decaying books for posterity, was not difficult. It was boring. Three slouchers in that undecorated capsule of a room all day long. But, per Sigrid, "everyone must have something to aspire to." And so they aspired not to cry.

Everything had an underwater feeling when Katherine put the headphones on. Michael cracked his knuckles each time he saved a document, and Sigrid sighed in immeasurable intervals. But under the headphones, it all felt distant, pressurized. Katherine imagined scuba diving, walking along the silty floor of the ocean, while the voice in her ears murmured about neuropathic stimulation of bonobos. Michael's clicking knuckles were a pod of dolphins far overhead, in conversation.

If Katherine had paid attention, she would have noticed that Sigrid sighed each time Michael cracked his knuckles. He never caught her drift. Sigrid checked the clock at least every minute. It was 3:00 p.m. She was hungry. The headphones were humid and tight on her ears. The clock in their typing closet was the kind that ticked. Katherine, beside her, typed like she was Mozart composing a symphony, and it was the time of day when Michael's jaw eased open and he began breathing through his mouth. She could smell it. She shut her eyes and thought of Marlon Brando. Or Humphrey Bogart. Marlon Brando or Humphrey Bogart grabbing her wrist. She turned up the volume of her headphones.

Katherine ignored Sigrid fidgeting beside her. She knew transcription was simple once you figured out how to stop listening. Listening was about understanding. Transcribing was about hearing. Her ears heard words and her fingers typed them. Katherine herself was hardly involved. A conduit doesn't spend time thinking of how it conveys. It sits in place and lets the current pass through. She would like to bring the headphones home. Isaac would think she looked like a NASA controller. She was monitoring fuel supply, oxygen levels, velocity, whatever it was they monitored. She was ensuring the well-being of brave astronauts crossing the bounds of human limitation. Sigrid rested her fingers on the keyboard. She hadn't typed a thing in at least an hour.

Sigrid and Michael, at day's end, looked tired. Michael yawned widely and Sigrid, with the look of a wilted flower, said she would skip her acting class and instead head home. Katherine felt as though she had just woken up from a long, dreamless nap.

"Or maybe I'll get a drink first," Sigrid said, thinking of the possibility that she might meet a man at a bar. As usual, what she said washed over Katherine and Michael. It was like they lived with headphones on.

"See you at home later, then," Sigrid said. She said "see you at home" each evening to Katherine as though there were a chance that they—coworkers and roommates both—might not see each other ever again. Katherine didn't fuss with a response. She raised her arms overhead and stretched.

At the after-school care center, Isaac was building a skyscraper with plastic pieces. Katherine sat down beside him.

"Hello," Isaac said. Katherine tugged on the hairs at the nape of his neck. His hair grew quickly and unevenly and he was starting to sprout a little brown tail there. He wanted to keep it.

When she came to pick him up, Katherine always let Isaac finish what he was working on. Isaac appreciated this about Katherine. That the other children were often dragged away in hysterics did not go unnoticed. Isaac didn't throw tantrums, reasoning that they were not worth the effort, never having yielded the results he sought. And in what he took as a sign of mutual respect, Katherine didn't do much that made him want to tantrum.

"Tell me what you learned today," Katherine said. She asked for this report every day. Sometimes Isaac hadn't learned anything, so he offered a fact recalled from one of his books.

"The largest organism on Earth is a grove of interconnected aspen trees in Colorado."

"Really?" Katherine said.

Isaac completed the skyscraper, and then, piece by piece, began to disassemble it. "They have the same roots."

For dinner: fried eggs on brown rice and carrot sticks.

Sigrid was in the living room watching TV, stretched out across the sofa, cheek at rest on the back of her hand as if she were a beauty in an oil painting, her body as tensionless as butter. Katherine didn't know if Sigrid ever ate dinner. She saw her sandwich at lunch—white bread and cold cuts with no spread or plant matter to speak of—but she never knew whether she ate dinner. Isaac was a generous child, often asking Sigrid if she'd like to join them, though Katherine didn't encourage it. Katherine had one person to take care of, and that was enough. Feeding a roommate wasn't part of the lease. But Isaac left some carrot sticks in a bowl for Sigrid, should she want to graze.

After dinner, Katherine balanced the checkbook and Isaac got out old magazines and scissors and glue and made collages of alien landscapes until it grew late. Then: bath time, reading time, bedtime, lights out.

Isaac took a bath, although, at eight years old, he felt he was old enough to take showers. He sensed Katherine might not want to see him growing up too quickly. Often, after dinner, he felt an urge to lean back in his chair and cross one ankle over a knee, but this seemed too adult a gesture for Katherine to witness. She might respond by baby talking or asking if he needed help with his homework, and there was nothing either of them disliked so much as coddling. He kept both feet on the floor. He ate the carrot sticks without prompting. He took his own dish to the sink and washed it and the other dishes. "He who is most self-sufficient is most at peace." Katherine had said this to him many times, had likely begun repeating it to him when he was in diapers. She would say to him, "Would you want to be seen as a person in need?"

She liked him to be independent, but she did not want him to be older than eight, and lamented each time Isaac needed to size up in clothes.

Isaac drew his bath, toweled off, brushed his teeth, and rinsed the sink of toothpaste.

"Goodnight," he said to Katherine, who was in her room putting on tights.

"Goodnight, Isaac," Katherine said.

Isaac knew not to say goodnight to Sigrid, who was still watching TV. His mother, he could tell, did not like him to. He wore a men's polo shirt as pajamas, a nightgown that went down past his knees. In bed, he read a biography of Abraham Lincoln. When he began to nod off, he turned out the lamp and went to sleep. He did not yet know that in one hundred pages, Lincoln would be shot.

In the living room, Katherine walked past the TV set and turned the volume down low. Sigrid didn't move, didn't even bother shifting her pupils from the screen. By now she knew it was easier to imagine that a wind had blown through the apartment and turned down the volume than to spend energy assigning any blame to Katherine. Katherine walked around with her chin tilted up and her eyes set on some far-off point, unable or unwilling to see what was right before her.

Wordlessly, Katherine left the apartment and walked the few blocks to the corner bar that was always nearly empty on weeknights. In these last few weeks of winter, the days had turned longer and warmer, the birds had returned and grown chatty, but the nights were still cold. Her legs, in her tights, were numb.

A young couple leaned against the wall outside the bar, smoking. They bounced their backs off the wall in an even rhythm that seemed choreographed, funny. Katherine felt them watch her walk by.

Albert had already set up the board at the bar. That night, it was backgammon.

"You won last time," he said, "so you get to roll first."

"Did I?" Katherine asked. The bartender brought her a seltzer with lemon. It was free, but she tipped a dollar. She rolled the dice.

"I sold enough piping today to stretch from here to the Grand Canyon." Albert said this in a James Bond voice for no apparent reason.

"That's very far," Katherine said. "Industrial?"

"Commercial."

Albert rolled the dice and talked about his day. Katherine pressed her knees and elbows to the wooden bar. Her legs had begun to warm.

"Are you a cat person or a dog person?" Albert asked. He had asked this before. He was drinking a gin martini. Martinis, Katherine thought, looked dignified in films. In real life, they came in small, twee glasses and were prone to being slurped. Albert didn't slurp, though. He wore button-up shirts and grew his hair a bit long and pronounced his name in the French way, *Ahl-behr*, though there didn't seem to be anything French about him. Every Monday and sometimes Wednesday for the last few months or so, Katherine wasn't sure, she had been coming here after Isaac went to bed, and Albert was always sitting at the bar with a board game. She suspected Albert came every night, playing alone or enticing a stranger to play, as he had once done with her. Albert was full of questions for Katherine, but her curiosity about him was not similarly piqued.

"I had a rabbit when I was small," Katherine said.

"I'm a dog person," said Albert. "I'm looking to adopt a German shepherd."

Katherine thought, I know, but didn't say it.

The couple from outside came up to the bar to order drinks. Albert was quiet while they stood one stool down from him, their hips pressed to each other's. They ordered two of the same beer. They looked like siblings, Katherine thought. Albert took his turn and moved his checkers.

"How was work?" Albert asked once they'd left.

Katherine shrugged.

"How many words per minute do you type now?"

"Still seventy."

"Pretty fast," Albert said.

Katherine turned to look at the young couple, who were caught up in each other in the back corner of the bar, sitting on the same side of the booth. The boy had his hand on the back of the girl's head, pulling her hair. Not hard, but persistently. The girl closed her eyes, her mouth opened. She may have moaned, but from where she sat, Katherine couldn't hear it. The girl reminded her of Sigrid, who struck her as a person who liked to be watched. And yet Sigrid stayed home all the time, where there was no one to watch her. Katherine had stopped announcing to Sigrid when she was going out and leaving Isaac, for Sigrid passed the entirety of every evening under the gaze of the TV. And anyway, Isaac didn't need to be watched.

When she turned back around, she realized Albert had been talking for some time about his apartment—where he would put the dog bed and water dish, the toy chest he would get for the German shepherd, how much less lonely his place would be then. Albert rested his arm against Katherine's beside the backgammon board. She wanted to, but she did not move her arm.

Katherine hadn't wanted a baby. She had been eighteen when Isaac was born, and though she loved him immediately, what she had experienced didn't feel like the love of a parent. It had been the love anyone could have for any baby—a biological imperative. For a long time, she felt that Isaac's true parents, out for the night at the opera, or in the other room preparing his dinner, would soon return to claim what belonged to them.

Now he was nearly nine and she saw that it was only that the baby came before the certainty. She had Isaac and so she had everything she needed.

In the morning, Isaac made six slices of toast, two for each of them, and put the butter and jam on the table. He was always up first. He preferred to eat his toast without scrutiny, because he liked a lot of jam on it. Gobs. Then came Sigrid, who ate her toast while she walked barefoot around the apartment, turning up the thermostat and pouring a glass of water and checking the time on the one clock that didn't run fast. Katherine was in the shower and emerged dressed, took her toast with a meager scrape of butter, and sat at the kitchen table with a novel opened before her.

Sigrid watched a few minutes of TV while she dried her hair, standing with the dryer plugged into the wall beside the console. She couldn't hear any of the dialogue.

When it was time to go, Katherine put on her coat and gathered her keys from the entry table. The jingling keys were like a bell ringing—they told Isaac and Sigrid it was time to go, without Katherine having to announce it each morning like a drill sergeant.

It was so regular that whenever Isaac heard other keys jingling, he immediately wanted to put on a coat. Sigrid wasn't sure why she felt compelled to leave the apartment with them but did it anyway. When the keys jingled, she, too, retrieved her coat from the closet.

They all left together for the subway. Outside, the day pressed in. It was the type of cold that makes a body fold into itself. Katherine and Isaac walked side by side, hands in their coat pockets, and Sigrid lagged behind, thinking of the TV show she hadn't been able to finish. She suspected the couple in the show would run away together. Not the two already dating, but the girlfriend and the other man, who seemed like he didn't know how to smile. All his frowning was what made it romantic.

On the train, Isaac held Lincoln's biography on his lap. "Am I a sickly child?" he asked.

"Are you sick often?" Katherine asked.

"No."

"Then no."

"You could still be president without the illness. If you wanted."

"Lincoln wasn't a sickly child," Isaac said. "Einstein was."

"Then you could still be a physicist."

"I'd rather be a biographer," Isaac said. He turned to Sigrid, who was standing three feet away, holding the metal bar. "Can I write your biography?"

Katherine shifted away to read the backside of a man's newspaper.

"My life hasn't even started yet," Sigrid said.

When was the last time anyone looked at me? Sigrid wondered this all day long while she typed a machinists' manual from the 1870s into her word processor. So many words were spelled incorrectly; she typed them as-is with a [*sic*] beside them. Someone had typed the manual on a typewriter perhaps two decades ago, and now Sigrid typed the text into a computer with a blue screen. One day someone would convert the text in another way that was as yet unimaginable. Flying cars, teleportation, little implants that let you read minds. Who knew what was over the horizon of the next decade, the next millennium? All progress one day becomes obsolete. Someone else would sort out the typographical errors. When was the last time anyone had looked at her? The night before, she had dreamed that a man followed her home. He was desperate for her. He wore a camel trench coat. He pressed himself against her, pinning her to a tree below their apartment windows. The bark was rough and sticky with sap.

The transcription room developed a certain smell by mid-afternoon. Michael had by then thrown a banana peel into the trash can. The three of them had shed dander, sweated, released some great number of exhalations into an enclosed space. Carbon dioxide. Isaac would know how many breaths per hour the average person releases. Or how many pheromones. What purpose did those serve? Sigrid's hadn't attracted anyone. Likely they were defunct.

Katherine was fastidious in her habits. Every hour within a ten-minute margin, she left the room and walked down the hallway toward the restroom. It was 3:03. Katherine rose and left. When the door shut, Sigrid turned to Michael. "Seen anything good lately?"

Michael removed his headphones. "What?"

"Done anything fun lately?"

Michael rolled his eyes up to the ceiling to think. Sigrid often thought of a sloth when she looked at him. He was good-looking in an oblong way, but she was certain most of the odor came from him. He had hairy knuckles and heavy breath. He was largely unknowable. He was the kind of person who thought before he spoke.

"No, I suppose not," he said. "Sasha has finals this week." Michael's girlfriend, Sasha, was in optometry school.

"Is she stressed?" Sigrid leaned forward in her chair, resting her chin on her hand.

"Yeah," Michael said. "She studies a lot."

"What do you do while she studies?"

"Stuff around the house, I guess," Michael said. "Our washer broke, and I had to call someone to fix it. Then Sasha wanted to put up some shelves, so I put those up."

"Wow," Sigrid said.

Michael went on, complaining about how there was nothing to watch on TV. So many commercials. Sometimes he spent a whole evening searching for something to watch, never finding anything.

While Michael talked, Sigrid pulled her hair down from its bun and let it fall over her shoulders. She shook it out, then twisted it up again into the bun, arching her back. Michael watched her, then the ceiling, her, the ceiling, her, while he talked about falling asleep in front of the TV. His eyes rolled, glassy and unseeing as marbles. He was not an observant person. Sigrid thought about unbuttoning her blouse, showing him her nipples.

Katherine came back in. Waxy yellow light filled the room and then faded as the door shut again. Sigrid gave Katherine a half smile, but Katherine looked right through her. As a child, Sigrid had been taught to speak only when spoken to, but Katherine hardly did even that. Sigrid stood and cracked the door to let in some fresh air. She sat back down and chewed on the skin around her thumbnail until it was soft and gummy, then switched to the other thumb.

They were in a windowless chamber on the basement level of the public library, which was beginning to lose a battle with mildew. Sigrid had always assumed librarians to be public servants, available among the shelves to translate Dewey decimal codes into locatable books. But the librarians hid belowground like moles, doing their own rote typing in rows of cubicles inexplicably segregated from the transcription room. Loneliness was made only more palpable when you attempted conversation with the librarians.

Sigrid had never seen a desert, but as she returned to the machinists' manual, wet thumbs on her keyboard, she pictured an aerial shot of herself wandering through one, alone, silk headscarf nearly carried away by the wind.

* * *

On the way to the bathroom, snug against a back wall, there was an indoor solarium that pulled in light from a ground-floor window above. Ferns, some real, some faux, were planted there in bark chips. Once, Sigrid had seen Katherine standing between the ferns, her blunt, home-cut hair looking very much like a helmet, gazing up through the cross-barred window as if she were staring across time and space into another dimension. As if she were a plant. Sigrid thought of that moment each time she considered speaking to Katherine. Friendship was a project she had long given up on.

When Katherine had offered Sigrid the room, Sigrid called Katherine her guardian angel. It was her first week in the city. She was living in a motel room and could not find an apartment she could afford. She had hugged Katherine for a long time, feeling her skeleton, small and slight as chicken bones beneath the overlarge knit sweater and floor-length skirt she often wore. A sob came bursting up from Sigrid's stomach. She imagined dinners together, ordering takeout, late-night talks. That Katherine had a small son at home was a surprise, but a good one.

"Isaac likes to keep to himself," Katherine told her.

"This is your room," Katherine said, while Sigrid followed her around the apartment. "This floorboard squeaks, but the rest are fine." She stepped on one spot of the wood, which did squeak. "You should avoid it."

The room was painted a startling white and had a bookshelf, and a window that looked directly across into another apartment building. Katherine gave Sigrid a set of keys. "Right," Katherine said. She shut the bedroom door with Sigrid inside.

At recess, Isaac played with twin girls, Maggie and Melissa, who looked nearly the same but who were nothing alike in manner.

Melissa was loud and would shriek sometimes for no reason that anyone could discern. Their teacher had called the mother in to talk about it, and everybody told Melissa she ought to stop getting in trouble, but she went on shrieking anyway.

In today's scene, Melissa was the opera starlet, and Maggie, who preferred the noble roles of mime or sculptor's muse, was the stealthy sniper who kept watch over Melissa's safety from a remote distance.

The fun part was setting up the game, not playing it.

Melissa would be on a train from Siberia to Paris, where she would soon star in the role of a lifetime. She would be practicing her grand finale when a thief boarded the train to steal her jewels. "My jewels!" she would scream, and Maggie, from behind a newspaper, would fire one precise and silenced shot to kill the thief.

Isaac was cast as the thief, but he didn't want the role. He wanted to be a scientist who would soon prove the theory of elastic gravity and discover a new planet in the solar system with an orbit so wide, it came into telescopic range only once every eight thousand years. The scientist would also be writing his own autobiography.

"What does that have to do with saving me?" Melissa asked.

"I'm just also on the train to Paris," Isaac said.

Melissa clapped her hands to her cheeks and pulled her skin down to reveal the red inner rinks of her eyelids. "That! Doesn't! Make! Sense!" She shrieked her usual shriek and then ran off to play with someone else. Maggie was over by the water fountain, tiptoeing around a corner with her finger gun raised high.

Isaac walked across the multi-purpose field, where kids played kickball and other sorts of loosely organized games that granted them an excuse to chase one another around. He gave the chain-link fence a kick and then stuck his arms through the links, imagining his hands in gloves handling plutonium from behind a four-inch-thick plexiglass wall.

*　　*　　*

Katherine tugged on Isaac's little tail. "What did you learn today?" she asked once they were settled on the subway.

Isaac looked somber, but it was sometimes difficult to know how seriously to take the troubles of someone whose feet swung beneath his seat when the train car veered. His cheeks were rosy from the cold. His eyelashes were long and thick as a doll's.

"How many black holes do you think exist in the universe right now?" Isaac asked.

"I don't know," Katherine said. "I don't think we have a way to know."

"But what do you *think*?"

"I think...," Katherine said. She remembered a magazine article she had read as a teenager, soon after the first black hole was discovered. A drawing of a black hole like a crocodile's eye. But how can you discover something if you can't see it or photograph it? She couldn't remember much in the way of facts about them. She wanted to say something funny like *one million trillion billion* or *all the fish in the sea times forty-six*, but she knew Isaac had grown too old for that. What would once have made him laugh he would now find patronizing. He likely knew the word—*patronizing*.

"I think scientists are developing a theory," Katherine said. "But probably many hundreds of thousands."

Isaac seemed satisfied. "There can't be too many, though," he said. "Or they'd consume the whole universe and us along with it."

"I suppose they would," Katherine said, though she didn't think it likely.

Sigrid, blond daughter of Dutch-born livestock veterinarians, had moved to this city because she wanted to do something important with her life. She changed her name back to Sigrid after seven years of opting to live as a Samantha. She subscribed to two fashion magazines. She pierced her ears. In this new city, she had taken voice lessons, modern dance, figure drawing, and printmaking, and now she was at the first meeting of a beginning acting class. It wasn't what she had moved to the city for. She'd once thought she might like to work in set design for theater. In each of her three years of college, before she dropped out, she had taken painting classes, and her final projects were often giant, storm-swept landscapes she liked to imagine stepping right into. Even when she set out to paint something small and foregrounded—half a lemon on a plate, for example, as was the assignment in her still life class —she spent all her time on the background, so that the wood-paneled walls and tapestry behind the plate were richly detailed, and the lemon was a bright yellow circle with no shadowing or foreshortening to speak of.

She wasn't a beginning actor, but the beginning acting class wasn't necessarily only for beginners. She had taken an acting class in high school and one in college, but this teacher taught a different method and so Sigrid was not beginning again but beginning something new.

In pairs, the class read lines from *Roman Holiday* while holding hands and thinking of the saddest thing they had ever experienced. Sigrid's partner had tears in his eyes, but Sigrid couldn't seem to think of anything sad enough. She thought of a girl from elementary school, two grades below her, whose mother had died of cancer. Sigrid had never seen the mother, but still, it was a terrible loss. All the children had made the daughter paper cards. She thought about crying. She felt her partner's hands, warm in hers, and a little sweaty. She read the lines from the script, which seemed to her as though they were meant to be romantic. She had never seen the film.

Katherine had never told her parents about Isaac. She was in her first year of college in another state. She had just broken up with a boyfriend and started seeing another boy, a sophomore from the next-door dorms. She didn't know which was the father and it didn't much matter to her, in the same way that it didn't seem like a matter for her parents to concern themselves with. She felt no shame at all, and her parents would not have shamed her. They were, by and large, kind and generous people, and her childhood had been happy, albeit pale and flat as the arid, tessellating farmland that surrounded their town. After modestly wilder years spent in intentional living communities, her parents returned to the place where they had grown up, to parent Katherine in earnest. Katherine was five when they'd moved and didn't remember much of the communes, but she had once found photographs of them in a drawer. Simple wooden A-frame houses and tents. Her mother topless, holding her breasts and smiling, a daisy in her hair. Her long-haired father standing beside a fire, arms raised like an upright bear. Now her parents had nearly identical short haircuts, her mother's set weekly in curlers. Those people in the photographs seemed entirely different from the quiet parents who had raised her, and she saw then that people were made up of the sum of their privacies. At the dinner table each night, conversation was careful and much like getting acquainted with strangers. It always seemed her parents felt guilty, whether for living in the communes or leaving them, she wasn't sure. Still, her parents gave her everything she needed. Not lavishly, but she had grown up easily and without want.

She didn't tell them about Isaac, simply because he was hers. Katherine finished the year of college, quite round by the end, told her parents she was taking a year off to work on a low-water farm in California, and instead enrolled in word processing school. By the time Isaac was born, she had her typist's certificate in hand.

At the corner bar, Albert dealt a game of gin rummy and Katherine tried to remember the rules. Albert licked his fingers as he portioned out the cards. Katherine's hand contained no sets, no runs.

"I called in sick today," Albert said. He left a pause, which Katherine filled by drawing and discarding a card.

"I wasn't sick," offered Albert.

"I'm glad," Katherine said.

"I checked in on my neighbor's cockatoo," Albert said. "My neighbor's out of town."

"What's its name?" Katherine asked.

"Sonora."

"Pretty," said Katherine.

After a long while warming up, Katherine took her coat off and set it on the stool beside her. Albert, she could tell, was looking at her. Tonight he drank a rum and coke with a straw. He didn't slurp. For all his attentions—the questions, the brushing up against her, and, tonight, a fresh shave and a dose of cologne—Albert struck Katherine as surprisingly passive in the face of romance. He had never flirted with her, never asked her out. They had met in this exact spot at the bar and there the acquaintanceship remained. They played tensionless rounds of gin rummy. Albert was perhaps ten years older than Katherine, had never married, had no children. Albert sold piping and wiring in what seemed to be a low-stress job. There were no products to push; builders either needed pipes and wires at the moment or they did not. Albert was sexless. He was thick about the middle, but that wasn't what made him sexless. Plenty of people were thick about the middle and sexual. Albert also had full lips and a square jaw and a dapper sort of haircut. But he wasn't sexual. It was something else he wanted from Katherine, something he had wanted for the many months they'd known each other. Whatever it was, Katherine felt no obligation to provide it. She didn't like for people to want—to want from her.

Albert laid down three sevens and a run of the two, three, and four of spades. Katherine had four aces, three queens, and four tens, but was keeping them all in her hand. Albert was nodding along to the song on the jukebox in a way that made Katherine think he was probably a good dancer.

As for herself, Katherine hadn't had sex since she'd learned she was pregnant with Isaac. She was now twenty-seven and felt fortunate to live without the worries that seemed to tie other people her age in knots: sex and marriage, stepladder careers, whether or when to have children. Katherine never needed to make another life decision. Things would go on as they were now for a very long time. She had Isaac, and he now needed little from her. He was, to her, immaculate and fascinating and entirely his own. She was Isaac's mother, and Isaac, for a little while, had lived inside her, attached to her. Now they lived their lives in tandem. She liked to think he had chosen to be born from her.

Albert was talking, still, about the cockatoo named Sonora, after the desert, because of her yellow and peach coloring, like a sunrise over sandy dunes. Sonora was four years old and wouldn't speak a single English word, though Albert did believe she understood the language. Sonora liked to chatter while she ate her sunflower seeds, removing seed from shell with just her beak and tongue in a way Albert thought was marvelous but to Katherine sounded like the thing that every bird did. Listening to Albert was like transcribing. Sometimes Katherine discovered she was humming while he talked.

Because Katherine had been thinking about Isaac, she said, "I named my son after a lake I lived nearby when I was young. Lake Palmer. It's a manmade lake, a perfect circle. A man named Isaac Palmer made it and then named it after himself. I don't know who he was, but I liked the name."

Albert moistened his full lips. "I didn't know you had a son," he said.

"He's eight," Katherine said.

Albert took a long drink of his rum and coke, emptying the glass. Then he looked at his cards for a while. He set down three twos. "Gin," he said.

Katherine still held all her sets in her hand. No points.

"I think I should have explained the rules better," Albert said. He was gathering his coat to leave.

"Bye," Katherine said, with a large ice cube in her mouth. She stayed and finished her drink.

Katherine entered the apartment as quietly as she could and checked to make sure no light came from underneath Isaac's door. He was, by this time, long asleep.

Sigrid was watching an old Lauren Bacall film in the living room, the volume low. She mimicked Bacall's gestures, holding her hands out to cup an imagined lover's face, mouthing the lines. She turned when she heard Katherine behind her, and it was as if Sigrid were inside the TV, looking out but unable to see Katherine standing there in the living room. Katherine looked at Sigrid's hands, cupped like mittens, and thought to herself that Sigrid was a ridiculous person. But at least she paid her rent on time.

Sigrid continued mouthing the lines, then turned back to the TV set once Katherine was back in her room.

When Isaac heard Katherine close her bedroom door and turn off her light, he flipped his lamp back on. Lincoln had been shot and all the gore of it would not depart his mind. To clear his thoughts, he read from an anatomy textbook, a chapter on the functions of the kidney, but that also struck him as gory. He thought of his own kidneys, at work cleansing his blood. Should one ever fail, he would need a transplant. As a concept it made sense, but the application seemed far-fetched. In appearance and behavior, people seemed all very different, and yet their insides were interchangeable. What, then, made Isaac Isaac and not Maggie? And how did Maggie's personality deviate from Melissa's, when their bodies looked so very alike? Somehow, they had once lived together inside their mother, fed and grown, as Isaac had inside Katherine. Bodies made other small bodies, and one day, no matter who made them, all bodies stopped working. Organs became ill or got used up. One at a time, or all at once. You could be shot, or you could grow old enough that there was no way to keep being.

Isaac had always thought of death as something like a trip to outer space. You floated. You rested in all that blackness, spinning like a planet or a star. It seemed peaceful. But when he thought of it now—the feeling of it, not a sleep but an absence, an unthinking, everything he knew and everyone he'd ever known, everyone who had ever lived, an undoing, an end—he stood up next to his bed, breathing hard.

"No, no, no," he said aloud in his bedroom, which was cold in winter even though he had shoved a towel at the seal of the window where the draft came through. It was a terrible thing. Isaac felt electrified, like he could run out the front door and up the street. But he made himself sit down on the bed. He put his palms over his eyes. He hoped his mother and Sigrid hadn't heard him.

Isaac knew well that happy thoughts could replace miserable ones. He played this game all the time at school, at the after-school care center, at home: Think of popsicles, of cartoons, of toys—baby things—and you will begin to feel better.

I will be nine soon, Isaac thought. By the time I am old, there will be a solution for it. Someone will have figured out by then how to keep on living forever. A pill. A serum. And so it is nothing to worry about. It isn't. It won't happen. He felt comforted.

When the film was done, Sigrid turned off the TV and went into the kitchen to heat up a bowl of soup. She liked to eat dinner right before bed, so as to fall asleep feeling sated and warmed from within. She ate and then moved toward the bathroom to brush her teeth. Down the hall, she saw that Isaac's light was on. Carefully, she opened his door. He was asleep with a book on his chest. It was draped over the sides of his rib cage like some overlarge set of armor. She didn't dare move the book, but she did cross the room and turn his lamp off. When she was leaving, she heard Isaac say, fretfully, "I was only asleep."

"And now you can go back to sleep," Sigrid told him in a voice she hoped was soothing. When she was small, she had suffered from nightmares, climbing into bed with her parents every other night. Perhaps Isaac had had a bad dream.

"Okay," he said. Or perhaps he was only talking in his sleep.

Earlier, Isaac had wandered into the living room with his tooth-brush in his mouth.

"What are you doing?" he had asked Sigrid.

She turned from the TV set. "It's for my class," she told him, though it wasn't. It was an exercise she had come up with herself

"Acting?" Isaac said.

"Mm-hmm."

Isaac went into the kitchen to spit out his toothpaste.

"My school is putting on a play," Isaac said when he returned, one foot perched on the arm of the sofa. He tottered.

"Oh, yeah?" Sigrid asked. "What play?"

"*Snow White.*"

"Did you try out for it?"

"No way," Isaac said.

"Bashful," Sigrid said.

"What?" Isaac was tugging on his toes.

"One of the dwarves. You would have made a good Bashful."

Isaac laughed, late, but sincerely. He didn't laugh often, but Sigrid could make him laugh.

"What are you trying out for?" Isaac asked.

"Nothing right now." On the screen, the camera panned across Bacall's tear-glistening face. Sigrid tried to tilt her chin the same way, to make her eyes sorrowful but her face as smooth, as creaseless.

"You could have been Snow White," Isaac said.

"Not the evil stepmother?"

"No."

Sigrid leaned over and gave him a poke in the ribs. "Time for bed, Sleepy," she said.

When Katherine was gone, Sigrid felt she ought to look after Isaac. Katherine made a point of saying she didn't need to, that he was entirely self-reliant, but Sigrid liked to care for him. Make him a cup of cocoa, play a round of Go Fish with him. Every now and then, if he was very tired or had a cold, he came out of his room and asked to be tucked in. It was something he only ever asked of Sigrid, something just between them that he did when his mother was out. When Sigrid played with him when Katherine was home, she could feel Katherine looking on disapprovingly.

They three had lived together for two years now. Sigrid was sure it was convenience and not kindness that had made Katherine offer the room to her when she arrived in the city as a college dropout with what was then a temporary job but nowhere to live, no furniture or basic toiletries. Here was someone who was helpless, with money to put toward rent. Katherine's previous roommate had left before the sublease was up.

In college, Sigrid's roommates had been her best friends. When she first moved in here, she baked cookies to share and invited Katherine and Isaac to watch movies with her. At work and at home, she tried every day to initiate a conversation with Katherine, whom she then thought of as shy. Sigrid had been shy when she was young, and she had grown out of it. At first, she empathized with Katherine.

Katherine was warm enough with Isaac. When she was with him, for the most part she released herself from whatever sleep she spent the rest of her days in. Most of the time, the only way to live with Katherine was to pretend she wasn't there, but still Sigrid couldn't help being polite. She stayed because of Isaac. In another life, she could have been his aunt. Snow White. It was the nicest thing anyone had ever said to her.

* * *

It was a slushy, snowy day at school, so there was no outdoor recess, no Melissa and Maggie, who shared a table at the opposite side of the classroom. Mrs. Cameron had tried to separate them at the beginning of the year, but the change had made them flip personalities, so that Maggie became fidgety and squawky, and Melissa withdrew into herself and bit her fingernails to the quick.

Isaac was tired. During Heads Up 7 Up, he put his head down on his folded arms and didn't pick it up again when it was time for "heads up." The cavern he had created for his face was warm with exhalation. He pulled his arms closer to seal the gaps and shut out the light. He exhaled long and slow and wondered how long it would take to run out of oxygen.

Mrs. Cameron came over and touched his shoulder. She was very sweet, and very pink—floral dresses, rosy cheeks and lips. It could have been makeup, but either way it suited her.

"Do you want to go to the nurse's station, Isaac?" She had a high, doll-like voice. Isaac sometimes wanted to hug her. Many of the children did, resting their heads against her hip, but Isaac was not accustomed to hugs.

The nurse put a thermometer under his tongue and took a look in his ears with that pointy black flashlight that tickled and prodded at the same time.

"Ahhhhhh," the nurse said, and Isaac knew to open his mouth.

"Tonsils are swollen," she said. She put a hand to his forehead. Medical hands were always so cold. "A bit of a temperature. Would you like me to call your mother?" the nurse asked.

"I would like to lie down for a little while."

The nurse put a sterile pillowcase on the pillow and Isaac lay across the green pleather mattress. Now he wasn't tired. He tried to count the holes in the perforated ceiling tiles, but they were too tiny—they wiggled when his eyes moved. There was a dusty stack of children's books on the bedside table, books that could have been at rest there since his mother was a girl. But he remembered she hadn't gone to this school. She was from somewhere else—he didn't know where.

The nurse had offered to call his mother, not his parents, and so she must have known Isaac had no father. There was, of course, a father, technically. Isaac understood paternity and conception. But when he, in a more curious phase, had asked his mother repeatedly who his father was and what he was like, she had responded only "I don't know." Nothing more. The mystery of it all had given him nightmares. He came to hope his father was dead, so that he would not be someone to wonder about. There was no wondering about the dead. And he hoped his father was dead so he wouldn't have to worry about him showing up one day and changing everything. Isaac liked things just as they were now, and so he had put an end to his curious phase.

When the nurse came by to check on him, he closed his eyes and feigned sleep. Later, when the bell rang to signal the end of the school day, he got up, went to the classroom to gather his backpack and umbrella, and stood in line with the other kids who, together with their appointed chaperone, would walk the three blocks to the after-school center.

Katherine suspected that the morning's snow had likely been a final showing before spring took over. Fat, wet flakes had plopped when they hit the ground.

Katherine had dropped Isaac at the front of his school with a wave goodbye. He dragged his boots through the sludge and in through the doors. Other children pushed one another into puddles and piles of sodden leaves or jumped, snapping at snowflakes like dogs after flies. Her child was dignified and serious and she appreciated that about him. She imagined he was already at his desk, opening his backpack and setting out the writing implements he would need for the day. He always completed his homework at the after-school center—she never checked to see if he'd done it. He earned exceedingly high grades, and if he didn't, well, it was his boat to row.

She walked the rest of the way to the library. If this was to be the last snow of the winter, she wanted to enjoy it. Katherine was not a warm-weather person.

Sigrid and Michael were already at their desks with their head-phones on, typing away. Sigrid looked up when Katherine came in after dropping Isaac off—a goodbye ritual that Sigrid was not invited to witness. Katherine's mouth was slightly open, as if she were going to say something.

"Hi," Sigrid whispered. Katherine nodded and sat down at her desk.

All three were working on different sections of a hypnotist and psychological theorist's patient sessions from 1948. These were all on records. The librarians had set up a record player at each of their ter-minals. After the transcriptions were complete, the librarians would transfer the recordings to cassette tapes to be scurried away into their hidey-holes. One day, people said, there would be robots to do this work instead of typists. She pictured a circuit board person much like a gingerbread man with fingers, typing away at her computer. Silly. Impossible. The thought made her smile.

Sigrid looked over at Katherine throughout the day. Each hour when Katherine stood up and left the room, Sigrid considered going after her and talking to her: Had Katherine noticed that Isaac was very tired that morning? He had risen from bed and dressed only after Katherine jingled her keys. His eyes were red and puffy. Did Katherine think something might be troubling him?

Katherine was picturing flying cars and escalators that took you up to the moon, while the psychological theorist asked his patient to imagine walking through a maze submerged in his mother's womb.

She didn't notice Sigrid's head oscillating toward her every few minutes. "Find the parting," the psychologist said. "Find the light."

"There it is," the patient said.

When Katherine picked him up from the after-school care center, Isaac did not tell her he had gone to the nurse's office that day. Instead, he told her about something he learned first thing in the morning, when Mrs. Cameron began class. On the overhead projector, she showed them images and explained the differences between asteroids, meteoroids, comets, and meteors, which were not to be confused with man-made satellites. If the storm cleared, they would be able to see a meteor shower that very night. It was reported in a newspaper article, which Mrs. Cameron read aloud to the class. Because of light pollution, the showing would be dim, but if the conditions were just right, they would see small beads of light streak across the sky.

Isaac told Katherine all about it. It was the only thing he'd learned that day and he wanted to watch the shower. Could they take the train to the northern part of the city, where the light pollution was not so bad?

"Of course," Katherine said. "As long as the sky clears up."

At home, Katherine chopped up a block of frozen spinach and added it to two cans of tomato soup. She and Isaac ate the soup with crackers.

"Meteors come through Earth's atmosphere," Isaac said, "but they don't leave a hole."

"Is that so?" Katherine said.

"But there is a hole. In the ozone. It exposes us to UV rays from the sun."

"You learned that in school?" Katherine asked.

"In the newspaper."

"Smart boy," Katherine said. "The most important things, you have to teach yourself."

"I know," Isaac said. He went on, "Sometimes meteors make it through Earth's atmosphere. Then they're called meteorites. There's a chance one could shoot down and hit you on the head, but not a big chance. No one has ever been reported as killed by a meteorite."

Katherine smiled at her son.

"But maybe if you stand right under the hole in the ozone layer," he said, "maybe then there's more of a chance. So you have to stay away from the hole."

Isaac stood and washed his plate and then went to the window to check the weather. It was dark now and the temperature had dropped. Snow fell more regularly, hard little specks on the black metal grating of the fire escape.

"Meteor showers happen more often than you'd think," Katherine said. "We'll keep an eye out in the newspaper for the next one."

Isaac pressed his face to the glass. He heard Sigrid come in the front door.

"Good evening," she said in a British accent. She came into the kitchen carrying all sorts of bags—groceries and shampoo and a betta fish in a plastic cup. She was wearing heels that clopped across the floor. She was breathless and smiling, her sheet of blond hair waving as she bent to unpack her bags.

"Hello, S," Katherine said. She had never called Sigrid that before—she hardly addressed her at all, really—but Sigrid let it roll off her.

"Oh, wow!" said Isaac.

"A fighting fish," Sigrid told him. "You can only have one, or they tear each other to shreds. Very territorial, they are." She switched back into the accent, more cockney this time. "He's for you. Want to feed him?"

Isaac sniffed the pinch of fish food, which smelled like everything but food. The betta snapped its jaw approvingly. Katherine was pleased, and not surprised, that Isaac washed his hands without being asked.

Sigrid was putting her groceries away—what seemed to be a two-month supply. "My acting class is very good," she said.

"You like your teacher?" Isaac asked.

"Oh, yes. And the exercises. I'm able to channel something now—something new. I've never felt it before."

"That's very good," Isaac said. He was balancing on one foot. He looked at Sigrid and then at his mother. He wasn't used to them being in the same room. "Isn't that good?" he asked his mother.

"Excellent," Katherine said. She stood to wash her bowl and spoon. Isaac had left crackers on a plate for Sigrid, but Katherine was now putting them back in the package.

"Do you think you'll go on an audition?" Isaac asked. He watched the two women orbit each other in the kitchen.

"I might." Sigrid was washing a cucumber in the sink, full of energy.

"I think I'll read for a while," Katherine said. Isaac was talking to the fish, and Katherine was happy he had forgotten the disappointment of the meteor shower. She shut the door to her room, lit a candle, and put a record on low. She was reading a novelization of the life of Catherine the Great.

Two hours later she emerged feeling as bold and sharp as Catherine. Isaac was now at the kitchen table reading with the fish.

"Goodnight," she whispered in Isaac's ear. She tugged his tail.

Sigrid sat cross-legged in front of the TV, hands on her knees, swinging her torso around in circles. She was watching *Roman Holiday*. Katherine put on her coat and then crossed the living room and crouched at Sigrid's side. Close to Sigrid's ear, she whispered, "You're not an entertainer. You don't need to entertain him." Then she stood and left, shutting the door quietly behind her.

She took a meandering route to the bar, though she was already later than usual. She loved walking in the snow, and the streets were mostly empty, save for occasional passing cars. She didn't particularly like the crowdedness of the city, but she did like the way it felt alive, attuned. Her skin and her mind felt active. She could see deep into the night like a big cat on the hunt. She was anticipating something, though she wasn't sure what.

Sigrid finished *Roman Holiday*. It was indeed a romantic movie, though what Katherine had said to her ruined the last half of it. She still felt angry. And she had been in such a good mood earlier when she bought the betta fish for Isaac.

In her bedroom, she tried on one dress and then another. She took them all off and changed her bra. She put on lipstick. She put the first dress back on. Sigrid could see low light beneath the frame of her door. While she readied herself, she heard Isaac taking his bath and brushing his teeth, and when she left her room, she saw that his door was halfway open. He was in bed reading an astronomy book, his blanket pulled up to his chin. For a moment, she thought she should stay home. But Katherine had told her so many times that Isaac didn't need to be watched, and tonight, for once, Sigrid had plans.

"Goodnight, Bashful," Sigrid said. "Don't stay up too late."

"I won't" Isaac said. He sounded congested.

"Do you have a cold?" Sigrid asked.

"No."

"Well, take some medicine before you go to bed. It sounds like you're getting one."

"Okay," Isaac said. Sometimes he seemed so adult to Sigrid— Katherine had trained him to behave that way—but just now he seemed very small. Still a babe, really, on the face of this earth and breathing for only eight years. Eight years. Could you even believe it? And they don't know how young they are, how brief a moment they've lived. Sigrid was twenty-two. She didn't know it either. She was on her way to meet a man for a drink.

*　　*　　*

Once Sigrid left, Isaac drank gulps of cough syrup from the bottle and went out to the living room to watch TV. He thought maybe the news would cover the meteor shower, but they were talking about gas prices and construction delays.

He felt the warmth of the cough syrup seep from his stomach to the tips of his arms and legs. He wiggled his fingers. He felt drowsy, but he didn't want to sleep. He changed the channel and watched two women and a man who wanted to be continents away from each other get stuck together in a broom closet. They stomped and stumbled and fell over onto each other in a way that made the audience laugh. At the end of the episode, he didn't feel tired anymore.

Sigrid was meeting her acting partner, the one who was able to cry so easily. He had asked her if he could buy her a drink sometime. He was a little older, she could tell, but probably not yet thirty, and it was a good thing, Sigrid decided, that he could cry like that. "Tonight. I'm free tonight," she told him.

Now, at the bar, he said the same thing again. "Can I buy you a drink?" Sigrid had a vodka and orange juice and her date, Rodney, had bourbon. It seemed like it might have been his second drink—he was already at the bar when she arrived—but definitely not his third.

"You look nice in a dress," Rodney said. And a few minutes later he said, "I like how you're wearing your hair." He looked a little like Gene Kelly.

They talked for a long while about their acting class, where they had both learned how to feel like someone else—really feel, as though they were inside another person's body and experience and voice. "It's so intense," Rodney kept saying. By the end of his drink he was quieter and smiling, a bit shiny above the brow.

"I think I'll start auditioning soon," Sigrid told him.

"Oh, yeah?"

"It's what I moved here for. I've always wanted to be an actor."

Sigrid had heard Rodney saying these exact words to another girl in class last week.

"Same," Rodney said.

"There's no purer art form," Sigrid said.

"So true," Rodney said.

Sigrid wished he'd compliment her again. She tried her best to look like Lauren Bacall. "In elementary school," she said, "I was in a play. I was Snow White, the lead. That did it for me. From then on, I've always known what I wanted to be."

"For me it was Iago, in college. I got the bug," Rodney said.

"*Othello*," Sigrid said.

"Yeah," Rodney said.

"Wow."

"It's just so intense," Rodney said.

It was Monday and Albert was not in his usual place. Katherine drank her seltzer and read the label of every bottle behind the bar. Albert always brought the game along, so she couldn't even play a round of solitaire to pass the time. She ordered another seltzer. She got up to go to the bathroom and saw Albert in a booth at the back of the bar.

"Albert," she said. He was sitting with a guy, playing some sort of card game, maybe hearts

"Oh, hi," Albert said. "How are you?"

"Good," Katherine said. They stared at each other for a moment, then Katherine said, "I'm on my way to the bathroom, actually."

Katherine peed, then went back to the bar. She took her coat and gloves off the bar stool and began putting them on. Albert came up beside her.

"I'm sorry," he said.

"For what?"

"I want to be honest. I saw you there; I was just with my friend. I didn't want to leave him alone."

"It's okay," Katherine said. She buttoned her coat, wondering if she had left the candle burning in her room. Albert stood looking at her expectantly.

"Are we friends?" he asked.

Katherine looked at his face. He looked upset and she wasn't sure she wanted to know why.

He said, "Look, maybe we could get together for coffee sometime and talk."

"Don't we get together here?"

Albert looked like a balloon someone was blowing air into. "It's just—" He blinked many times. "I was surprised when you mentioned your son the other night. You've never said anything about him. In, what, a year of coming here, you've never mentioned him."

"Yes," Katherine said. She stood as still and straight as a pine. Could it really have been a year?

"You know so much about me. I didn't understand why you would keep something like that a secret. It didn't feel right."

Katherine thought for a moment and then said, "We can get coffee," she said. "It's a good idea."

"Okay, I'd like that," Albert said. "Friends?"

"Yes," Katherine said. She reached out and squeezed Albert's arm. She could tell it was what he wanted her to do. He looked confused, but happy. His lips were, Katherine thought, really very full. In an unpleasant way. "Next week sometime," she said.

Outside, the snow had stopped. Isaac looked up between the buildings to see if the sky had cleared. It was 10:17, just past the peak of the meteor shower. With the glare of the streetlamps at eye level, he couldn't tell if the sky had cleared or not. He cracked the window that opened out to the fire escape and looked up through the metal grates. Too obscured. He opened the window all the way and put one foot on the sill, then pulled the foot back inside and went and got his sweater.

The night felt soft and hushed, damp from all the melting snow. Isaac lowered the window nearly all the way, leaving a gap for his fingers to wiggle through. There was just enough space for two small feet on the fire escape, which was stacked with flowerpots, all empty or inhabited by dormant twigs. Isaac scooted them around to make enough room to crouch. A little plastic pot fell to the ground below, scattering soil. They were only on the second floor, so the fall was not impressive.

Isaac looked up. The sky was cloudy, but maybe a gap would open up. A perfect window to the stars. He wanted to get closer. He began to climb up to the fifth floor. The metal railings were rusty, but the steps were solid and didn't shake. He passed easily by the other windows where people seemed to already be asleep or sat resolutely facing their TVs, backs to him.

Getting onto the roof involved swinging his leg over a waist-high parapet and rolling from there onto his stomach and then onto the flat bed of the roof. He stood and looked up. Cloudy. The air up here was breezier, but not significantly colder. The buildings surrounding theirs were a story or two taller, so he couldn't see the span of the city, but he did see a big piece of sky. He put his hands around the back of his head to support the weight of it as he stared upward, willing the clouds to part, until his neck began to feel like it might get stuck that way, so then he chose the driest place he could find, a knoll of tar paper, to lie down on.

Sigrid thought about sleeping with Rodney. She was having such a good time with him, and the way he was looking at her suggested he liked her. Really liked her. She was very happy just now—someone had invited her out, had asked her questions about herself that she'd had to think through before answering, had pinched her fingertips between his when she left her hand on the table for exactly that purpose. This moment was nice, before he asked anything of her. If she could, she would stay in it forever. But men always asked something of you, and that was when you had to decide what exactly it was you wanted. It was better to be wanted than to want something yourself. Then you didn't have to know what to do. And he did seem to want her. Really want her. She finished her last drink slowly and let Rodney lean in to kiss her. The orange juice in her glass had warmed to room temperature and it tasted watery and candy-sweet. She liked the thought of her mouth tasting so sweet to him.

The snow had stopped falling and Katherine was disappointed. It had all but melted and was now beginning to freeze as the temperature dropped. She watched the sidewalk for ice, hoping it would snow one last time before the weather changed. The walk cleared her thoughts. No one was out and the air was all hers to breathe. People were asleep or settled in wherever they would pass the rest of the night. Even the brick buildings seemed like they were sleeping. She made her way home, stepped silently up the stairs and into the apartment. It was cold inside. Sigrid had left a window cracked an inch. She could be so careless. Katherine shut and locked it.

Down the hall, Isaac's light was out and his door was slightly ajar. Katherine left it open, thinking perhaps he wanted to hear her come home. Sigrid's door was closed, and her light was out. She, too, was asleep.

Katherine's candle had filled with molten wax and extinguished itself. Her record player had reached the end of the record and stopped of its own accord. She undressed, got into bed, and remembered the conversation with Albert. He said she knew a lot about him. But what did she know? He sold commercial and industrial piping. He told her he lived somewhere in the same neighborhood. He wanted a dog and a cat and a bird, but his landlord would not allow it. He had been raised in a far-flung suburb, by a mother at least, if not both a mother and a father. When they first met, he had just returned from a trip to the Philippines, where he had sold piping and seen rice terraces and gotten food poisoning, but not too badly. He had lost someone close to him, and many of his friends were sick. He told Katherine he wanted to sit somewhere where he didn't know anyone and play a game. These last details Katherine recalled now. It wasn't that she had forgotten, but she didn't often think of him when they were not together, and so she had put what now seemed to be important facts about Albert on a shelf somewhere deep in the vault of her mind. Albert had mentioned these details the night he first approached her, but not again. "I'm not here to hit on you," he said. He had held a deck of cards. If they really had been meeting for more than a year, it was longer than she usually continued on with people. They'd had hours of conversations, but those half dozen things were all she could recall. People seemed to need this, Katherine thought. They needed people to know many facts about them in order to feel like the relationship was real and worthwhile. But Katherine didn't feel that way. What pleasure was found in revealing oneself? Quite intentionally, Katherine had not indicated when and where they would meet for coffee. Albert had no way to get in touch with her. It would disrupt her evening routine—where was another quiet bar?—but she would simply never go to the bar again and that would be that.

Isaac sat up. He wasn't sure if he'd fallen asleep or if he'd been staring so fixedly at the sky that he'd forgotten where he was. The city was quiet and there was a break in the clouds. He could see a few stars and the hazy light of the moon's dim glow low on the horizon, but no meteors, comets, or satellites. Isaac thought of the North Star leading sailors home. He stood and made his way to the edge of the roof, lifted his leg over the parapet, swung over onto his stomach, and landed with an echoing bang on the fire escape below. He looked down through the metal grating. Each window below was dark. Down he stepped, holding the rusted bar lightly—he didn't want rust poisoning. It was close to or below freezing and ice had frozen in patches. His body felt rubbery. Perhaps he was getting a cold. He could feel his blood moving through him, slow, heavy, extra-susceptible to gravity. He shifted from step to step like he was wearing leaden boots.

When he reached his own balcony, his knee buckled, then sprang back into place. He kneeled on the outer ledge of the sill to open the window, which was shut now, and found that the window was stuck. He shoved it with his shoulder a few times. He knocked on the pane, lightly, and then hard. No one came. His mother must still be out. And Sigrid?

He could wait for his mother, watch the front entrance. She never stayed out that late. He could drop to the ground and wait at the door, but the drop now seemed very far. He could hang by the lowest bar of the fire escape, swing forward, and kick the doorbell panel, ringing each and every buzzer so that surely someone would come down and find him. But he figured his legs weren't long enough for this. He knocked on the window again.

He sat down on the balcony, his sneakers tucked between two towers of flowerpots. His pants were wet from the roof and clung to his skin. Shivering was the body's way of keeping warm, so he exaggerated his shivers to try to warm up. He drew his head into his sweater for a while, letting his breath warm his face, but then he worried he would miss his mom coming home. He watched. He knocked again.

How late was it? Where was it his mother so often went? His ankles felt colder than his feet. What did that mean? What percentage of blood was iron? Did your kidneys struggle to cleanse your blood if your blood was cold? What happened to an eyeball when it froze? Was outer space this cold, or colder? The meteor shower, it would have looked like snow coursing right across the sky, not so different from the snow that had started up again—white bits visible as they fell in front of the dark windows across the street. It was nearly the same as seeing the shower. He thought of going back up the stairs to knock on another window, but all those people were asleep and it seemed a careless thing to do to ask them to wake up when his mother would be home soon. "He who is most self-sufficient is most at peace." He began to feel warmer. Like he was in bathwater. If you stepped into the sea and let yourself float, it would take you seventeen months to reach land again. He would sleep for ten minutes, and then he would begin to shout until someone found him. In the morning, he would tell Mrs. Cameron he had seen the meteor shower and she would smile in her pink way.

Sigrid had the cab driver drop her two blocks away to save on fare and then walked the remaining distance. She pulled her scarf over her head. Snow was falling again. She hadn't gone home with Rodney. He had told her he lived near the bar, but not suggestively. He gave Sigrid a lingering hug and then let her go on her way. They'd see each other in class next week. He had walked off without turning around to take another look at her.

Now she was tired. It was late. She had work tomorrow. More time with her head pinned between two speakers.

A plastic flowerpot lay on the ground in front of her doorstep. She kicked it into the gutter. She looked up.

At first, she thought it was an animal or a burglar crouching out of sight. A black lump on the balcony. But that wasn't right.

"Isaac?" She said it once, then repeated it louder.

Two fingers poked through the balcony grating. She could see his nose and his eyes, expressionless, watching her put the key in the door.

When she got him inside, his pants and sweater were stiff and frozen. She got his clothes off him and sat him right next to the radiator, wrapped him up in blankets, and made him drink a cup of hot milk. Sigrid was quiet, tiptoeing. She didn't ask Isaac what he had been doing outside in the snow or how the window came to be locked. It was important to be as quiet as possible. They should not wake Katherine. It felt as though the pair of them had done something wrong together.

When Isaac stopped shivering and began to return to himself, Sigrid let him give the betta fish another pinch of food. He whispered to the fish, "I saw the meteor shower."

She sat him on the edge of the tub and began to brush his teeth for him. "Where were you?" Isaac asked Sigrid. His toothbrush was in his mouth, but Sigrid could understand him.

"I had an audition," she said. Isaac had two adult teeth in front, but the rest were almost too small to brush.

"Did you get the part?" Isaac asked, spitting out the toothpaste.

"Yes," Sigrid said. "I went out to celebrate after."

"Congratulations," Isaac said. His eyes were already closed. "You will be a very good actress."

Sigrid dressed him in his pajamas and tucked him into bed. When she was bent over, her ear very close to Isaac's face, he said, "We won't tell my mother."

ECLIPSE

by KIRSTEN SUNDBERG LUNSTRUM

THIS IS HOW I FIRST saw her: I was standing on the shore. It was an early spring morning, but gray. This was not long after the light disappeared for good. The sky was the color of my grandmother's pewter pitcher, or the inside of an oyster's dirty shell. Where heaven met earth, some alders made a rickrack of black lace, and fog topped the water like the layer of fluff inside a new bottle of pills.

Imogen was the first to step out of the waves—bathing cap first, then white neck and arms. When she took off the cap, her pale braid fell down her back. She had the high step of a seabird picking its way across the sand.

It took a minute for the other girls to separate themselves from her, one after the other slipping out of Imogen's body, like a deck of cards splaying in a fan, or a paper chain unfolding. One, two, three, four—they kept falling from her, until soon they were all visible, the whole company of eight girls, identical and standing in a line on the rocky stripe of beach.

Other than my mother's, they were the first ghosts I'd ever seen.

*   *   *

Unlike Imogen, I live on land. My house is four rooms and a porch. It has wood floors and a fireplace, a kitchen that smells like onions, a bay bush growing by the back door. It's at the end of a dirt road on the western side of an island on the western side of a continent.

My house is not really my house. It belongs to my grandmother, who is not my grandmother but is the woman my mother called Mother. She is small and wide-set and strong. She can cut a cord of firewood in one day's work. She can sew a dress just my size, measuring only with her eyes. She can bake a loaf of bread that tastes like heaven. She is faithful to me and to God above all else. My grandmother wears her still-dark hair in a chin-length blunt cut, the same as I wear mine, because she's the one who takes the scissors to both our heads. She likes to say, "Blood isn't what matters," and this is what I told Imogen that first day on the beach when she asked why I wasn't afraid of her. "Blood isn't what matters."

Imogen lifted her slim hand and struck it hard against the black barnacles that crust the beach rocks. Her skin split—a little fissure— but only a fine strand of white grains poured from the cut. "I'm made of salt," she said.

I shrugged and offered her the hem of my skirt to wipe her palm against, but she put the gash to her lips and sucked.

"Like Lot's wife," I said. She didn't know the story, and so I told her: "There was a woman who had to leave her home. God told her, 'Don't look back,' but the woman couldn't help herself. When she looked over her shoulder and saw her town burned to ash, she was transformed into a pillar of salt." I nodded at Imogen. "Now you tell me something."

Imogen frowned. Even then, when we were new to each other, I could read her thoughts as if they were printed out in neat script. I could see all of her and—through her—all of everything else.

"Once," she began, "there were two girls—sisters—born at the same time."

"Twins, then," I said.

"Of a sort. One sister was born of a mother in the usual way. The midwife lay the infant in a crib near a window, and as soon as the sunlight fell through that window and onto the first baby, the second baby was born, her sister, a shadow."

"And?" I asked.

"And what?" Imogen said. "That's the story."

"Nothing's happened yet."

She smiled, shrugged her cloudy shoulders. "It's what I can tell you now."

This was unsatisfying, and for a moment I was irked at her for hoarding the story.

"Let's skip rocks," she said, though, and as if she'd been hoarding them, too, she handed me a palm full of perfect skipping stones, each of them gray and wound round with one white band.

At the edge of the water, where the foam piles up white-brown like a lip of bubbled milk, we stood shoulder to shoulder and threw in our stones. They broke the skin of the water and sent out even ripples, one circle erupting from the next, before the hole sealed over again, slick and still, steel gray as our sky.

There are too many ideas about our darkness to name them all.

"For at one time you were darkness, but now you are light," I have heard the pastor read at church. And also, from Matthew, "The sun will be darkened, and the moon will not give its light; the stars will fall from the sky, and the heavenly bodies will be shaken."

Meanwhile, the scientists talk about an obstructive body. "Imagine a lake of dust," they say, "floating in orbit between Earth and the sun."

Perhaps it's ash, some think—the result of a volcanic eruption on a distant planet.

More believe we've done this to ourselves, our waste a cloud-veil that covers the sun's face during the day, and at night obscures the moon and stars.

I don't yet know what I believe.

Soon, my grandmother tells me, if the light doesn't return, the grass and the flowers will stop growing. The trees will stop putting out leaves. The wire-bramble of blackberries that fence the road leading to our place will stop fruiting, and the animals will disappear. I know this, but it frightens me to hear her say it.

Already, the tourists have stopped taking the ferry to our island. No one wants to pay to see a beach in the dusk. No one wants to stand on the corner by Queenie's Market and eat ice cream in the chill of the afternoon's darkness. The summer houses along the beach road have all been shut up, and the stores are closing, too, one by one, because there's just not enough business to keep the doors open. Even longtime island people have left—the man who delivered our mail for years, Ms. Vorlean from the bookstore, my teacher. There are empty houses on every street, and the people who haven't left mostly stay inside now. Fear grows where there's no information, my grandmother says, but it doesn't make sense to me why the school had to close, why the library shut its doors. The only place you can still go is church, which I suppose some people find comforting.

"We'll be fine," my grandmother says to reassure me. "We have our faith and we're resourceful, you and I. We'll manage."

I wonder, though. Our backyard garden did poorly this year. The potatoes were the size of walnuts, the carrots small and pale. And the rabbits and deer completely devoured anything aboveground, they were so hungry. My grandmother has a pantry full of canned goods still, but I know we'll eat through them quickly once the rest is gone.

"It won't be forever until the light returns," my grandmother says again and again. "Everything has its season and every season ends." She kisses me on the head just as she kissed my mother the night she disappeared. One kiss on the crown of my head.

Sometimes I feel the strength of the kiss run down the center of my body like a stake going right through me, a peg, rooting me to this place.

Other times I think she's a dowser and the kiss is a rod, testing me: *Is there anything of value left here in this body?* the kiss asks. *Has this girl gone empty yet?*

Not yet.

Imogen soon became my only friend. Sometimes I passed the houses of my old friends on my way to the beach. Behind their closed curtains, the blue-green lights of televisions flashed. They wanted to stay in the old world, I realized. One where the difference between day and evening was more than a change of grays. They wanted glare and squint. Heat on the cheeks and shoulders. Sunglasses and burns. The sparkle of a reflection playing off someone's wristwatch, or the square of afternoon light unfolding on the floor beneath the window. I knew because I wanted that, too, but for me watching it flattened on a TV screen would never be enough.

The other truth is that those children hadn't ever really been my friends. Their mothers knew about my mother well before I did, and they didn't want her influence in their homes. That's the way my grandmother said it to me: "They don't want her influence in their homes," as if, like my shadow, my mother trailed behind me always. No one had ever been cruel, but they avoided me, and so I became used to being alone.

Maybe this is why Imogen seemed so wonderful to me. I wanted to be with her, in her presence, all the time. As soon as my grandmother freed me from breakfast to run outside, I went to the beach. I couldn't call to her—the water between us would only swallow my voice—and so I took to standing on the sand, still as a heron, watching the water for signs of her. When she did finally spot me, she'd emerge from the sea like a person climbing up a staircase from a basement, head, shoulders, torso, legs. Behind her, her sisters always followed.

One afternoon a few days after we met, I asked, "What does it look like below the water? Is it just darkness there too?"

We were sitting side by side on a tumble of bleached driftwood. The sand flies jumped like fleas at my feet, more sluggish in the cooler temperature than they used to be. I shooed them away. Behind us, Imogen's sisters had arrayed themselves along another log, one girl in front of the next, all of them focused on grooming one another. I watched them finger-combing tiny shrimp and bits of seaweed from one another's hair. Next, they'd set to work on their elaborate braids. This was their routine.

"Is it dark at your house too?" I asked again.

"I don't know how to answer that," she said. "Yes and no."

She told me about the plankton that glittered like stars. At night, she said, when even the little light from my sky overhead disappeared and the surface of the water went true black and endless, only then was it possible to see them—tiny animals, each an ember. They moved in currents, she said, like ribbons of light threading the waves. Like the veined band of the Milky Way. I pictured it. We'd lost our moon just like our sun. We'd lost all our constellations.

"Bioluminescence," I told her. "It's a chemical reaction." I explained what I had learned in sixth-grade science class, before the light left, when I was still going to school. I was good at science, and I loved it. Wasn't science, after all, just asking questions? We learned about motion and energy, the solar system and the atom. We made simple machines from paper tubes and rubber bands and coat hangers. We built atomic models, egg-suspension inventions, and balsa-wood boats that we sailed in a plastic baby pool in our classroom. I remembered it all now the way I remembered so many of the details from life before the light left—like my mind had all along been a storage room in which I was hiding things away. I'd forgotten what was in there until the darkness outside forced me to turn on the lamp and look around.

I told Imogen what I knew about bioluminescence—about fireflies and lantern fish and siphonophores, which look like single jellyfish but are actually colonies of many organisms. "They use the light they make to camouflage themselves, or to speak to other animals. It's a code they can signal with their bodies."

"Colonies?" she asked. She tipped her head the way a listening animal might do, frowned. The feathered gosling-gray down of her eyebrows furrowed.

"Communities. Groups. Many rather than one."

"I know the word," she said. "I meant why."

I repeated my teacher's words: "They work together to keep the whole body alive."

"Like my sisters and me," Imogen said. The girls all turned their faces to her at the mention. "I require them, and they require me."

"I don't understand."

"I require my sisters. All of them." She looked at me with her pale eyes and took my hand in hers. I could see our skins touching, but I felt nothing.

I thought of how, when I was a little girl, I liked to climb into my mother's bed in the morning. She had the bed that is now mine and kept it in the room that is now mine too—the east-facing bedroom. When it was out, the sun always fell first through her bedroom window, and lying beside my sleeping mother, I liked to pass my fingers into and out of the square of light the window cast on the quilt. Light/dark. Warm/cool. My mother's hand/my own. The light was both nothing and not-nothing on my skin, just like Imogen's grasp.

"Are you here or not here?" I asked her.

"Here."

"And when you go back into the water?"

She smiled. "Is the sun gone just because you can't see it?" She pointed up and I followed her finger. The sky was thick, the color of wet sand, a cave wall. I couldn't be sure what lay beyond it.

"I don't know," I said. Again, I thought of my mother. She left in the middle of the night. The last time I saw her, she hit my grandmother—struck her across the face. She'd wanted money, and my grandmother said no. The pills my mother took had made her sick and thin and pale, a parallel and sometimes violent ghost of herself. "I don't know," I repeated.

Imogen's fingers laced between my own. "You know more than you think you do."

Later, once Imogen's sisters had folded back into her like a string of paper dolls stacking and she/they slipped back into the waves, I walked home in the dark, moving my arms in front of me as if I were swimming, too, my fingers combing the cool air, pushing me forward, forward, forward through the trembling cone of my headlamp's single beam.

It was early summer when the ferry stopped making its run between our island and the mainland each day. We'd been without sun for six months by then, and without sun we were without tourists, and without tourists there wasn't enough revenue to pay for the fuel. The state's department of transportation suspended all ferry operations. A few more island families gave up, packed their belongings in crates, and got on the last boat leaving. Several of us went to the dock to see them off.

My grandmother's friend Lena was one of the departures. She had a son on the mainland, and he'd offered to make room for her in his house. At the boat that morning, seeing Lena off, my grandmother looked puffy-faced and weary. She and Lena had known each other since they were girls. "She's making a mistake," my grandmother said as she waved to Lena, who had climbed aboard the boat, disappeared, and reappeared a few moments later on the upper deck. "She'll see. It will be worse over on the other side."

"You think so?" I asked. I wasn't thinking of Lena so much as my mother. We didn't know where she'd gone when she left, but it was somewhere on the other side.

"Oh, yes. Yes, I do." My grandmother had put a cotton scarf around her neck as we'd left our house, and its blue and yellow flowers seemed shockingly bright against the gray sky, white boat, brown wooden dock railings. I was still getting used to seeing in sepia. I wasn't sure I ever would.

"Why do you say that?" I asked. "What have you heard?" But my voice was drowned out by the blow of the ferry's low, keening horn and the sudden thunder of its massive engines churning to a start. I leaned over the dock railing and watched the water roil, a skirt of frothing white bubbles and rolling waves ruffling outward from the ferry's hull. I thought of Imogen and her sisters there under the water, the massive body of the boat like a shadow, but white. It reminded me of how, in the days when the sun rose and hung at the apex of the sky, passing clouds cast shadows onto the fields. These shadows moved like barges over the tall grass on a summer day, real and not real at once. Maybe that's what boat bottoms looked like to Imogen and her sisters. Maybe our whole world was little more than shadow to them, the way they were to me. On the dock, I put my clammy fingertips to my arm to check for my own materiality, but there I was—skin and bone and fine blond hairs—just as always.

"You okay?" my grandmother asked me.

I nodded, and she took my hand, and we walked home together.

That night, I couldn't sleep. Before I closed my eyes, I thought of my mother—not as a woman, but as a little girl. Wild eyes and stringy hair and dirty feet. Girl abandoned and alone, found in an empty house on the south side of the island, screaming like a feral cat. My grandmother had claimed her body and kept that safe, but you can't claim someone else's fear. That had stayed with my mother always. I fell asleep thinking, You can't claim someone else's fear, and so I dreamed fear. In one dream, I was on a boat made of paper and rowing for my life, but before I could reach the shore of the mainland, the water dissolved my boat's bottom, cold water rushing up around my ankles. I woke with a gasp, certain that my feet were wet. When I finally fell back asleep, I dreamed of another boat, only this time it wasn't me on board, but my mother, looking as she had before the sickness took her, her face still full and beautiful, her long hair and yellow dress blowing behind her with the sea breeze. I called to her from the beach, but she had no oars, and the tide was pulling back from the lip of shore, her boat drawing farther and farther away from me until soon she was just a bright, golden spot out on the horizon. This last dream was vivid, and I couldn't shake the film of unease it left behind in me, and so I got up and went to the kitchen for a piece of bread to settle my stomach.

My grandmother was sitting at the table. Only her hands and the embroidery hoop she was holding were lit by the orange circle of the lamp's light. "What are you doing up?" she asked.

At the counter, I cut myself a thick slice of the bread she'd made that morning and buttered it. I thought: There won't be butter much longer. I was angry with myself for thinking it. Why did every thought have to be trailed by its negative now?

"I can't sleep," I said.

She made a grumble of sympathy. "Sit with me."

I pulled my chair out from the table and watched her sew as I ate. Her fingers whipped tiny knots into the white fabric. A picture of a forest was rising on the surface of the cloth. Evergreen and lime and goldenrod and blue. Trees and wildflowers and the spotted outline of a stream coming into being, one knot at a time.

"Do you think we should have left too?" I asked.

"No," my grandmother said without hesitating or lifting her head. "We live here."

What I wanted to say but couldn't swelled like weather inside my chest. I opened my mouth and took a breath to speak, changed my mind.

"You don't have to tell me," my grandmother said. "I know what you're thinking. You imagine I don't miss your mother? Worry about her? And now Lena too." She clicked her tongue, sound of disapproval and disappointment—at their choices or our circumstances, I wasn't sure.

"No," I said. Fury flamed to life in my gut. I felt myself turn torch, turn conflagration. My face would light the house. I touched my cheeks, took a breath. "No," I said again. "Why should we worry about the people who chose to leave? I'm only worried about us."

My grandmother set her embroidery in her lap and we sat together in silence for a long time.

"Look at the birds of the air," she said. "They do not sow or reap or store food in barns, and yet they are fed." It was what she'd said to me when my mother left. I remembered.

"Go back to bed now," she said. "One of us, at least, ought to get some rest."

I put my plate on the counter and went to the room that is my room but was my mother's. I lay in the bed and looked up at the ceiling, which was flat and blank and as airless as my body felt. Ash. Char. Salt. "Goodnight," I called to my grandmother, not because we were usually so formal, but because I needed the sound of her voice returning to me.

"Goodnight, my love," she called back.

The next day I woke groggy, bleary-eyed, and in a bad mood. I wanted to go immediately to the beach and to Imogen, but it was Sunday, and my grandmother was up and dressed and waiting for me when I stepped out of my room. "I let you have a lie-in," she said. "Service starts in half an hour, though, so get moving."

On our way to church, we saw that a metal chain had been strung across the entrance to the ferry dock, and boards had been nailed over the windows of the ticket office.

"Well, we're stuck now," my grandmother joked. She was wearing her black dress—the one she wore to church every Sunday. Its fabric was dusted with white stars, and its skirt billowed and whirled like clouds of smoke around her shins as we walked. Overnight, her sorrow seemed to have hardened into a resolve about our own survival. "We have enough flour and corn and canned goods put up to last us through next winter, even if they do close the grocery," she said. "We'll be fine."

Speaking certain thoughts aloud also speaks their inversion. In saying, "We'll be fine," my grandmother cast the words *We won't be fine* like a net around us.

At the church, there was only a handful of people seated in the pews. Pastor Geraldine shook our hands at the door. "I'm glad to see you're still here, Willie," she said to my grandmother.

"Where else would I be?" my grandmother asked, and the pastor smiled.

The service was short but felt long. The pianist had gone off-island in April, and so we'd been singing the hymns a cappella. Our voices dragged and tugged at one another, out of time and out of tune. In my head, I pictured the Portuguese men-of-war that now and then washed up on our beaches—each one actually a colony, and all of them together a stranded flotilla of blue sails on the sand. I pictured the corals of Australia, and the writhing stream of millions of sugar ants I'd once seen climbing the side of a house. I thought of flights of bees and swallows. Hives of cities full of people, all bumbling through the daytime darkness in confusion. *Require* was the word Imogen had used. "I require them," she'd said of her sisters.

In English class, before the darkness, we'd learned about collective nouns, the way they name a community. The water was part of Imogen's community, just as her sisters were. And the piano and the ferry and the sunlight and my mother had all been part of mine. What happened when a colony divided, split? What happened when, like voices dropping from the scale of the chorus one by one, the members of the community vanished? What would become of one without the many?

From the pulpit, Pastor Geraldine read the scripture. It was the story of Noah from the book of Genesis. "And every living thing that moved on land perished—birds, livestock, wild beasts, all the creatures that swarm over the earth, and all mankind. Everything on dry land that had the breath of life in its nostrils died. Every living thing on the face of the earth was wiped out." All but Noah, Pastor Geraldine told us. She described a drowned Earth. Trees and mud and houses swept up by the floodwater. Sky and sea reunited and as endless as they'd been before God swept a hand over the world and divided them, dark from light, dirt from stream, chaos into order.

I closed my eyes and pictured it. Light from the sky falling on the water, a salting of jewels. I saw Noah's boat cutting through the waves and leaving behind only its blazing wake.

"As long as the earth endures, seedtime and harvest, cold and heat, summer and winter, day and night, will never cease," she read. She looked out at those of us gathered and nodded.

It's a lie, I wanted to say. *It's all ending. It's all ended.* But from somewhere in the front pew, a voice sang out the first note of the closing hymn. When it had finished, my grandmother touched my shoulder. The cluster of us who had gathered then stood and shuffled out into the dim late morning.

After the service, I convinced my grandmother to let me skip lunch. I wasn't hungry. I couldn't have eaten if I'd wanted to. Some Sundays, I felt the words of the scripture pour like cool water over my head. On those days, I could walk out of church with peace still fresh on my face like dew on the grass in the morning, and all day I could feel its slow evaporation off my skin. But today, I was still ablaze, nothing settled in my head or my gut.

What I needed to understand was where the light had gone. When Noah's flood washed over the earth, the land did not stop existing. It was there, under the water, waiting for God to invert the storm and draw back the curtain of sea. Where was the light now, then? In my science class, we had learned that light is energy traveling from the sun, and that in a closed system like Earth's, energy cannot be created or destroyed, but can only change form.

I considered this as I walked to the beach. If our light had been covered, like a candle beneath a basket, it was still there, on the other side of whatever was separating us. If it had been converted, transformed like water into ice or steam, its new body could be found and returned to us.

The only true end would be a betrayal, a theft—God cutting a hole in the heavens and reaching through to disappear the sun in his fist. God the destroyer.

I didn't want that God.

I ran to the beach. I felt the heat in my face and thought: Energy. If I could keep running—run all the way around the island again and again and again—could I light myself up? I imagined my face like a lantern, incandescent, illuminated and illuminating. "May God's face shine on you and be gracious to you" were the words of the benediction Pastor Geraldine used each week to send the congregants out into the world. As if the sun were God's face, now turned away from us, and from the misery we felt at this absence.

"Imogen!" I yelled when I reached the shoreline. "Imogen! I need you!"

But this time, she didn't emerge from the water. It was thick and placid. Here and there, where a blade of kelp or a bit of washed-out driftwood bobbed, a pin-tuck dimpled its matte surface, but it remained otherwise undisturbed, the beach empty but for me.

I could wait, I thought, or I could go to her this time.

I pulled the knots of my shoelaces, peeled my socks from my feet like damp fish skins come away from the flesh. My dress, which was too small for me now, I had to wrestle from my body, and once I was free of it, I flung it down in a blue heap on the rocks. I stood in my underwear, my tank, nothing between me and the water but a few feet of sand.

I had swum in this sea many times. My mother had always told me I'd been born in it, though I wasn't sure I believed her. "I felt you were coming," she'd said, "and so I walked down to the beach and stood in the water. It was August. It was so hot. The cold and the waves took the pain away. I needed to take the pain away." These things she whispered into my ear when we lay together in her bed, now my bed. The sun was warm on those mornings, pouring into the room through the window the way water pours from a faucet. I felt it fill the spaces between our limbs as well. It glazed my mother's face in honeyed light, her freckles pink-orange spots on her cheeks and nose and forehead and chin, her hair the color of strawberry milk spread out on the pillow. My mother's skin always smelled like sweat and ginger, tasted like salt.

Now, at my back, the wind nudged me out of my memory, pushing me forward down the beach. I stepped around the barnacled rocks. Under my weight, water welled up, fanning out in dark stars on the sand. A rill of goose bumps lifted along my spine, my arms.

"Imogen!" I called again. The water licked at my toes, my ankles. I pushed my feet forward until they disappeared. The brown-white foam locked around my shins. My knees tingled with the needles of cold. I thought of the ice-fur I'd seen form on the windows of our house in midwinter. I kept walking out. The fabric of my underwear soaked through and clung to my skin. My stomach clenched tight against the cold. Now I was in as far as my ribs, my heart. I lifted my feet from the bottom and let the motion of the waves drift me out. "Imogen!" I called.

*   *   *

Here's what else I remembered:

My mother left before the light did. It was summer, so there were hours and hours of extra light; in fact, the days were long and the sun only thickening—pinking like the inner flesh of a melon—as it sank over the edge of the island and melted into the sea.

I knew nothing of my mother's life outside our house, except that she lived more and more of it there—wherever *there* was—and less and less with us. I'd go to sleep alone in the bed we shared, but wake in the middle of the night to find her returned to me, sleeping curled against me, her skin sweating a spicy smell, her breath sweet like rotten fruit. She slept in her clothes or in nothing at all. When she was naked, I could see the puckered skin of her belly. I'd left her that way when I'd escaped her, she told me once. I'd left her ugly like that. But I didn't find her belly ugly. The skin there was pale and soft and wrinkled. It gathered around her navel the way fabric gathers when snagged, as if in letting me out of her, she'd had to unravel something of herself. I liked to lie next to my mother when she was sleeping. She was not dangerous asleep. She slept the heavy sleep of an animal, sighing now and then but never waking—not even if I touched my hand to her belly, where I'd once lived. Not even if I put my ear to her chest to listen to the sound of her breathing, as if my mother's body were the shell and she were the secret ocean deep inside it.

That last night, she did not come home for dinner, did not come home to tuck me in. It was my grandmother who combed and braided my hair after my bath, who read to me, who put me into bed and kissed my forehead goodnight. "Goodnight," I said, but when she left I got to my knees and parted the curtains and watched the road, waiting for my mother to appear.

I don't know how long I waited, but at some point I fell asleep. When I woke again, it was dark. The sun had gone down and my mother had finally come home. It was her voice that woke me. Her voice like an ax blade on the other side of the bedroom door, bright and hard and angry. Screaming. "Shame," she said. "Wickedness," she said. "Bitch." Words with silver teeth.

I sat up, swung my legs over the side of the bed. Welt of light swelling around the bedroom door. Sound of a dish breaking. Sound of a woman crying, though I didn't know which one—my mother or my grandmother.

"Grandma?" I said.

It was my mother who had thrown the dish. She stood across the room, her back against the wall. She was wet and dripping dark splots of water onto the rug. Her hair clung to her head. In her face, her eyes were caverns. Her mouth a dark red hole. And through her thin T-shirt, her nipples were inky stars.

"Go back to bed," my grandmother said.

"Don't you tell her what to do," my mother said. "Don't you tell her. You're not her mother. You're no one's goddamn mother."

Like a comet, she was across the room. She hit my grandmother. One swing.

I don't know if I remember this next piece or if I've invented it, but my mother looks at me. She looks at me, and she is and is not my mother. She is changed. She is standing in front of me, her hand still in the air with the motion of the strike, and she is also at the same time already gone. She is also at the door. She is walking away. Which is the real mother and which is the ghost? I can't be sure. She has split, though, divided. She has peeled one layer of self from the other, and the one still looking at me is dissolving like salt in water, and the one walking out the door is a shade of grainy dust.

"If you go," my grandmother said, "you don't come back."

And that was the end of it. She turned away and went.

My grandmother touched her fingers to her face where my mother had struck her. Split skin beneath her left eye. Smear of blood.

"You're hurt," I said.

"Doesn't matter. I'll be fine. We're both fine."

*   *   *

Inside me, my lungs constricted. The farther out I swam, the harder I had to work to pull in a breath. Water lapped at my neck, at my earlobes. When it entered my ears, my head exploded in white light, and I stopped moving—I must have stopped moving.

Under the water, it was like night. My eyes burned with the salt. Gray and green and brown. Flecks of plant matter and sand stirred up by the motion of the waves and long strands of slim seagrass like hair.

Imogen?

But she didn't appear.

Imogen?

I was too cold to swim, but I lifted my face and held my eyes open against the sting.

Bright blue sparkler trails. Fists of glitter tossed into the waves. Iridescent veins.

My head throbbed with the cold, and my throat—my throat ached.

Imogen?

My grandmother's voice fell like a whisper through the batting of the water.

I reached up my hand and broke the surface.

What I know now is that there is always going to be the time before. I used to be afraid of it following me. I felt it like an animal whose leash I could not let go of, like crows roosting in the trees just over my shoulders.

"We are made of the same dust," my grandmother has said. *We* meaning all of us, but—I always added silently to myself— particularly those who share our blood. At one point, I was part of my mother's own body. A stitch in her side, and then a swelling in her middle. It was only her body that kept me safe. I was heart and lungs and brain and bone kept on this side of death only by the thinnest barrier of my mother's own body. And that's not much, when you really think about it—muscle and skin and bone and blood. It returns to dust just as easily as it manifests from it.

When I finally told this to my grandmother, the night I almost drowned, she bent down and kissed my forehead. I was on her lap, like a little girl again. "It isn't blood that matters," she said.

She had carried me home from the beach on her back, stripped me of my wet clothes, and wrapped me in a blanket the color of flame. Now she held me, warming me with her own heat.

"No," I agreed. "I know that. It isn't blood that matters."

I thought of Imogen and her sisters. They required one another, and I required them—until I didn't. What had happened to me in the moment the cold had rushed in? Floating there, under the water, I had thought: I am nothing but a shadow. I saw myself dissolving. I would disintegrate. I would be the particulate in the water's current. I would trail the bellies of passing boats, a wake of saline lace. I had closed my eyes, ready. But then, stars.

Overhead, as I hadn't seen them since the darkness began, trails of blue glitter. Where the water snagged and pleated and unfurled itself again on the surface, constellations assembled and dispersed, realigned elsewhere. The world had flipped, swallowed me or lifted me, or both. I let out the last of the breath I'd been holding and watched the bubbles, each outlined in blue light, rise. I stretched out my arms and followed them up to where my grandmother was reaching for me.

"I saw the bioluminescence," I told my grandmother.

"Isn't it beautiful?" she asked.

"You've seen it?"

"Of course. I've lived here all my life."

"I thought it was the sky. Just for a minute."

She shrugged. "One thing isn't that different from another."

"It made me happy again, until I hit the surface and realized."

"There's nothing wrong with being happy," my grandmother said. She kissed my forehead again and pulled the orange blanket closer around me. It was a comfort to be held.

I thought: There's always going to be the time before, but there is also now.

Outside our windows, the gray of late afternoon was thickening to the silt-dark of dusk. Not a star was visible. Not yet.

FIVE
SHORT
STORIES
by
HEBE
UHART

*Translated from the Spanish
by Samuel Rutter*

JULIA

ONCE THERE WAS A woman called Julia who was friends with all the liars. Because she loved them so much, and she wanted to make them happy, she told huge lies too. And everyone was happy.

And even though the woman called Julia is dead, all those liars who were her friends still say: "Let's go see Julia this afternoon and chat for a while."

COMING *and* GOING

THE TRAINS CARRIED PEOPLE who were coming and people who were going. When people were going, they would throw open the windows and poke their heads out, and because it was early, the sunshine was magnificent and you could see morning glories all through the countryside. Sometimes they crossed paths with the people who were coming back. Those people were bothered by the sun, which is why they kept the windows shut tight, propped their heads up on their elbows, and stared out at nothing in particular, their brows furrowed. The people who were going would stare at them in curiosity, and sometimes a kid would yell goodbye, but the people coming back never answered. Sometimes one of them would smile with great sadness. Those who were coming back got off the train, their arms full of packages, then walked off into the distance and were never seen again.

After that, the train filled back up with people who were happy to be going, and they opened all the windows so they could see the countryside bathed in sunlight and covered in morning glories.

The FLY

THERE WAS THIS MAN who was always making speeches. He'd talk about what had improved and what had gotten worse, about life, about the fact that we all have to do our part, and also about the prosperous nations. This man would raise a finger and his eyebrows, too, whenever he spoke, and sometimes he lost his temper.

Once when he was talking about everything we had to do and slamming his fist on the table, a fat blowfly began buzzing around him. And this was a guy who just loved chasing flies. All of a sudden, he stopped talking about everything we had to do, and we looked around at one another. The man stalked the fly and tried to corral it, keeping at it until he caught it. Then, as soon as he'd caught the fly, he went on talking about all the things we had to do.

The BOOK

HERE'S WHAT IT SAYS in the book: "If you ring a doorbell while saying the word *toro*, and at the same time a red car drives past, you will die."

It was two o'clock in the morning when she rang the doorbell and said the word *toro*. She heard a car go by in the street and ran to see what color it was. The car was already off in the distance and she thought it was light brown, but she couldn't make it out clearly. She went home, sat on her bed with her head held high, and said, "Toro, toro, toro."

JUDAS

"WHEN I GET TO THE mountain," said Judas, "I'm not going to look at the orange tree." First, he passed a barren field; he felt honorable and majestic. He reached the mountain, and when he passed by the orange tree, he didn't look at it. For a moment he thought he could feel the resignation of the world emanating from the mountain itself. Full of gratitude, he looked up: the orange tree was by the side of the path, next to a small plant.

FROM ABOVE

by AMANDA AJAMFAR

THEY LISTEN AT THE gates of Heaven, sneaking around outside those high garden walls, tendriled and pockmarked where vines have crowned the tops of the barriers and spilled over, growing downward. They wait to hear the secret words, sacred chants, divine gossip from within—and then they drop crazily to Earth, their eager tongues pressed to their teeth to keep from writhing. They search for the humans who will listen. When they reach that willful, rebellious, unafraid heart, they whisper the precious sounds, give the stolen magic freely. Harut and Marut, the fallen angels: even after all these years they make that titanic round-trip over and over as though strapped to some terrible wheel. *Smash* into the walls of Heaven; *smash* into the ground of Earth.

They are propelled by pain. Hurt feelings. So they had fallen for her, that human woman Zohreh. She was also made by God, wasn't she? And who were they but the most obedient angels, to resist what God made irresistible? They did not blame her, exquisite lady, for using what they'd revealed—in pillow-talk ecstasy, the most sacred of secrets: the ineffable name of God—to ascend to the heavens. What was a human but something that God made weak and wily? She had asked them what would happen if she repeated the name, and they had admitted their ignorance. "It's never been done," they told her. "What man would dare try?" they asked. And the consequences were not so awful; she is still lovely there, affixed in the firmament. Zohreh, Venus. But He, so angry when His games don't go the way He wants—He punted them from Pairidaeza.

Harut, the more furious, the more hurt, had aimed to offer that most powerful utterance, the one Zohreh had used, to all men. Let them fill the sky and leave Earth and Heaven barren—a loophole in His plan. But the two angels found mankind resistant. No other humans were yet willing to do as Zohreh had done: to take their own place in the sky and forfeit any chance of closeness to God. To be apart from Him, eternally. It is a terrible freedom, desirable only to those who wish to destroy the sacred bond of creator and creation—to break the heart of God. Even those who would stray, would do the evilest things, were not willing to make such a final choice. The humans would take only lesser magics and use them uselessly in small, human ways: kill the neighbor's flock, grow their own fortune, cure the sick—petty parlor tricks. Marut consoled his angelic brother: "We'll just keep trying. Someday they'll want it. We have eternity." And so, because what is damned has nothing better to do, they did. Unforgiven and unforgiving, they fanned the flames of their anger and threw themselves into the task.

The old woman, Maryam, has no memory of feeling sincere faith, not even from childhood. Born poor into a crowded family, she had felt only the smallest flutter of resistance in her heart when the first angel offered her power. It had been Marut who found her, a child of twelve, scabbed knees, an empty stomach, and a wild, wounded pride that far outsized her body—all of this had caught the angelic eye.

"I can tell you how to stop the blood," the angel offered. "And how to make it come. How to keep a woman from dying in child-birth, and how to make sure she does."

Maryam had taken everything the angel offered, and called him down when she found herself wanting more. Marut grew annoyed with her neediness and so Harut took over. Upon their first meeting, when she was still a young woman full of brittle strength, he had thought her worthwhile. The rage she housed in her small body, which refused to grow no matter how much it ate, seemed prom-ising. But over the years Harut began to see the limits of her. The anger that had so impressed him was revealed to be thinner than he'd thought—only a matter of temperament, a lingering effect of the fear that scarcity and neglect breed. Harut stopped tending to her so closely, visiting only every few years. The last time he had seen her she was cancer-ridden and nearing her mortal end. He asked if she would consider the final blasphemy. The woman had laughed at the angel.

"I have not been perfect, but I still know my place. God has willed this all. And for that I am grateful, ya'allah."

And so he could not argue, Maryam cackled and coughed her way through the many names of God—the ones man is meant to know—until the angel left. Harut vowed to return to her only at the very last moment, when her suffering was at its greatest, on the off chance that the moment would change her.

Now, feeling that that moment is near, Harut drops from his perch in the sky, aiming for her faint, familiar heartbeat.

Wind still whistles over the metal body, though there is no soul inside to hear the sound. It is a terrible thing, not meant to touch the bosom of the sky. Angels, birds, even clouds passing by cannot understand. How can it move without consciousness? What humans have done, what they do, is getting so grotesque. Creating things that do not live but exert and consume as though they did? Terrible. An affront, surely. Someone should do something about it.

The appalling *thing* opens its not-a-belly and drops not-a-baby, but a littler thing like itself, moving with precision but no awareness, and that littler thing whistles all the way to the ground. When it strikes, *smash*, it blooms up and around, tearing everything it can reach.

Harut, falling from a greater distance, almost pulls back. But even an angel cannot stop a force like falling, so still he lands, *smash*, on Earth. The ground is up in the air and moving, all the pieces of buildings and cars and people intermixing. Harut waits for it to settle, immune to the heat and whipping force. He searches for Maryam and finds her gone, completely, his dim chance missed. Though sixty-three years of tending the woman was barely any time at all to the angel, and his hopes had not been high, he still feels cheated by the loss. He feels great rage, for a moment, toward the *thing* that swept in so suddenly to tear his plans apart—but it is such a foreign object. So bloodless a thing, for all the carnage it brings, that the angel knows nothing on Heaven or Earth that can harm it.

Turning his attention back to his mission, his knowing spreads, looking for the kinds of mortal hearts he needs. Once, long ago, he might have spent this time differently. He might have reached out to all the screaming, tattered little pieces of life beside him, tried to roll them all together and comfort them—but not anymore. His mission is no longer to offer ease to the hysterical creatures of Earth.

Arman, a mortal man, sits watching his sheep. They had been spooked by the explosion, still noticeable, though some distance away, but he lacks the energy to calm them. So they baa and bunch together, stepping on their own babes, panicking one another. Arman's young grandson, Paiman, waits to see if his grandfather will take charge. When he does not, the boy walks out among the animals, lightly slapping their plushy backsides, and, raising his voice in the firm, smooth way he has learned from his grandfather, soothes them. Though the sound had come from the southern horizon, the child keeps his eyes on the empty sky, where he knows the missile came from. The sheep calmed, he looks to his grandfather for an indication of what they should do about that too. Finding none, he acts as any helpless creature might when there is unknowable danger in the sky: he tucks himself under a scraggly tree and keeps his gaze upturned.

Arman is trying to remember the words to a song from his own childhood. It is what he does whenever that distant, dull thrumming starts from high above or a thud like blast reaches across the land. He thinks it would be nice to die with a song on his tongue—one that is familiar and well chewed. He knows it is indulgent to turn inward while Paiman sits there, wanting his help and comfort. It is easier for the old man; death is coming from within or without soon, anyway, but for his grandson he knows it must be harder. The poor boy will either die young or learn to live like this.

As Arman tries to come up with something to say, some verse or quote for Paiman's distress, he feels a tickle in his ear. He jams a thick finger into it and pulls out a wad of wax, greasing the white hairs sprouting there. Still it tickles. He sticks another finger in, trying again to clean it out. But now the tickle is a sound instead of a feeling. A voice, strange in pitch and accent—and perhaps there are some plump lips bumping against his earlobe, maybe even warm breath on his cheek?

"Jinni?" the old man asks in a low voice. His grandson, still straining his eyes upward, does not hear him.

"No, not jinni." The voice seems offended.

Arman waves his hand at the air near his ear, empty, though still he feels the breath and lips hovering.

"Away, shaitan. I have nothing for you." But he says it meekly. Even Arman would acknowledge that he doesn't cast the devil away as strongly as he should, not these days. His thoughts, once clean and pious as could be, have for a long time now been churning with doubts and cruelties, become congealed and clouded.

"Don't lie, old man. You can't hide your heart from me. I come bearing gifts."

Arman shakes his head and his turban begins to fall. He feels the breath, the lips, leave his ear, and as they do, Arman also feels his heart call out, missing the warmth and the touch of the sacred, if profaned, being. It returns. The man looks over to his grandson, obscured by the tree, and sighs. He knows it is dangerous even to entertain blasphemous thoughts, but he has always followed his own heart, believing it to be where God resides. Now that it is so inclined to hear the words of this invisible creature, he cannot let the chance pass to speak to a being of such knowledge.

"Not in front of the boy. Come to my home tonight, after the family has gone to sleep. I'll think about your gifts then."

Harut is angry that this mortal thinks himself special enough to deserve an appointment. But as the old man carefully unwinds and rewinds his turban, his cataract-clouded eyes steady on the small black plume rising from the south, Harut sees clearly the expression of Zohreh, like a ghost or shadow, in the old man's features. Though the face is entirely different, the shape of the eyes and set of the brow, the angel recognizes this type of weariness, a mix of strength and pain. A millennium ago, Harut had not known what it was, what it meant, how precious and powerful it was. He sees now that it is tender, this way of being for the human, and that it might still recede, become simple exhaustion or sorrow. The angel decides that he will be patient, nurturing. He will warm the man until what is inside is ripe, until it breaks open and spills out, so extraordinary and bittersweet.

As the sun sets, they arrive home and shut the sheep in their pen for the night. Even in the low light, Arman watches Paiman move through the motions so well learned: how to step among the animals, how to speak to them, how to hold himself. The boy is still small but already contains all he needs. This is calming to see, sweet to feel. Generations, Arman thinks. I have guaranteed generations. But even as he thinks this, he knows it is a lie. Nothing is guaranteed; there is only God's will. This refrain, one he has used often in life when he remembers to humble himself, is so much less comforting than it once was.

"Babaei," the boy says, pulling Arman's sleeve. "Do you think it would be good to put a light here, in the courtyard?"

"For the sheep? They can see fine. God gave them all the sight they need."

"For the planes, so they can see it is just sheep here. They won't make any mistakes, maybe, if they can see our house better."

"Hm." The old man considers the boy's idea. "Perhaps it's best that they don't see us at all. Maybe we shouldn't turn on any lights at all when the sun sets."

"They'll see us anyway. They have those..." The boy pauses, then uses English words that Arman does not know. "*Night-vision goggles* and *sonar*. They just need to see better so they know we are not doing anything."

Arman is confused by this line of reasoning, but cannot argue about what he doesn't understand. He pats the boy on the head. "Ask your father what he thinks."

The boy shakes his head, which is still under his grandfather's palm.

"He won't listen to me, but if you say it..."

Arman does not answer the boy's unfinished question. He will not intercede, because he does not want a hand in damning them—he is so unsure of which is better, to be seen less or more, but he will not let the boy know that. He simply keeps patting the child's head until they reach the door of their home.

Throughout dinner Arman watches his family with the feeling of being a stranger. They are quiet, tired, and overburdened, but still his daughter-in-law is full of care for Paiman, making sure he gets the largest chunks of meat, that his plate is full. Arman's wife tries to keep the mood light, telling the same little jokes and stories she tells every night, the ones that everyone knows and laughs at with gentle effort. When Paiman mentions the blast they heard, the boy's father makes up comforting lies, claiming to have heard it hit only an empty building, saying that the strikes will be moving away now, that they're losing interest in the region. His daughter-in-law mentions school starting soon, how proud she is that Paiman is going to be attending again this year. She turns to Arman and asks, leadingly, if he won't miss the boy in the field. Arman knows he is meant to praise the boy's skill, his helpfulness, but also to voice his own pride in and approval of the schooling. He moves his mouth to do this but finds only weak coughs pouring out.

His wife pats his back and mutters prayers and jokes at the same time, puns and rhymes to cover her concern. They clear the meal, plates, and tablecloth without expecting Arman to help, to move at all. He sees how clearly they are resigned to his distance, to his lack of effort, and he knows it is largely out of love and respect—for his age, his years of hard work, his right to rest—but he feels that it is also out of weariness. They have noticed the changes in him, but they are too fearful and tired to press him. They all try so hard, every day, to speak around the thing, the truth that takes up all their thoughts, that keeps their heartbeats fast and fills their vision with haze.

Any moment, even the quietest ones can turn into infernos. Humble before the will of God, yes, Arman thinks as he watches them move around their home. That is what we have always been. But this enormous, constant, endless fear of annihilation—this is not what man was meant to live with. No faith can conquer this.

Walking across the room with blankets piled high in his arms, Paiman catches his grandfather's eye and smiles, flashing a candy in his mouth. Arman smiles back instinctually but feels tears well behind his eyes. The boy is good, so good, and yet no amount of goodness will save him.

Harut makes small circles in the dust as he waits in the tiny courtyard of Arman's home. Far above, beyond human eyesight but well within Harut's purview, the metal *thing* is moving, too, watching too. Neither of them was ever meant to exist on Earth as they do, and so both have unnatural sight. Yet while the not-an-eye of the *thing* can see only human warmth moving within the house, Harut sees also love, worry, pain, and disease as they move through the humans. He watches the family exist in their animal patterns; they touch one another and feed together, and even from this distance Harut can hear the gurgling and sloshing in their stomachs, the flowing and straining of their blood, the little electrical buzzes and snaps in their brains. He sees an embolism waiting patiently in the head of Arman's wife, and the slow clotting of his son's heart. The angel considers telling the old man that his daughter-in-law's spirit is fracturing, full of cracks—the poor thing will not last the year. Only the grandson is whole and vibrant, though even he trembles in ways that nothing so young should. If it could, the *thing* above would be jealous of Harut's sight, his ears, his nose. If it could, it would imagine the possibilities of such surveillance as limitless and complete. If it could, it would recognize the angel as exactly what it hopes to, one day, in perfection, be.

Watching the mundane tasks of the humans, Harut feels his attention pulled to memory. Zohreh, her smell and her sound. She was only a mortal woman when they met, but Harut could swear that she was different from the rest. Her eyes brighter, her heartbeat louder. Though they had been disguised she had known they were not men, and still she took them to her bed with neither fear nor awe. Their presence on Earth had been a test of angelic virtue. With Zohreh, Harut and Marut failed over and over again. When they offered her their little magics, she took each one with a laugh and tossed it away. Back then, Harut had not known humans well enough to realize how cruel her laughter was, how unamused. He mistook the red of her cheeks for exhilaration, didn't know yet that it could be fury that widened a human's smile. When they told her the secret name of God, she had wept, and they thought it was a natural response because they knew no better. The way she had changed, then. The way she jumped from their arms and ran into the night. Harut now casts his gaze upward to her, untouchable and enduring.

The lights go out and the breathing of the family changes, their hearts slow, except for Arman's. He neither relaxes nor sleeps as Harut watches him through the walls. After some time, the old man slips out of bed and enters the courtyard, walking past the angel, to sit on a little chair in the far corner, across from the sheep pen. In his hands is a copy of the Qur'an, closed.

"All right, jinni. I'm ready to talk."

"Really, you just need to listen." Harut has spent hours planning which stories he will tell, the arguments and examples and honey-sweet words he will use to gloss the path for rebellious human thoughts. He puts his lips to the man's ear.

"No, no, I have some questions." Arman taps the book in his lap.

Harut thrusts his tongue out and presses it between his lips to blow forcefully into Arman's ear, sending angelic spittle flying. The old man jerks away, clutching the offended organ.

"What makes you think I want to answer your questions?"

Arman keeps his hand over his ear, but still he feels the breath, the lips.

"I'm seventy-two, never once missed a prayer, never invited your kind into my life. Now, as soon as I... begin to have doubts, you appear by my side. You've been waiting for me."

Harut cannot deny that he has been waiting, though he would never have guessed he was waiting for Arman. It is not unusual for humans to turn as they age, to become more angry or desperate as that final moment—always known, never believed in—approaches, but rarely is the human as virtuous as this one. He will not use the magics trivially to take revenge on some traitorous family member, or to fortify his body for last-minute debauchery, or even to prolong his life. His intent is purer than all that, his hurt is finer. It is like Harut's own, and that means it is worth everything.

"What do you want to know?"

Arman chews his own tongue, wanting the words to be right, thinking of all the old stories of mischievous jinn and tricky, whispering shaitans. He knows this creature to be evil, a traitor to God, but he hopes it is not just looking for laughs.

"When I was a younger man, I could hope that the men inside those machines"—he points a finger straight up at the sky—"would stop if they knew what they were doing. They never did—but that didn't matter. I had hope. I kept faith in God's will and in God's mercy." He pauses, keeping himself from praising God, biting the instinct in his tongue. Doing so, for the first time in his life, causes a strange stabbing sensation in his heart, but he only places his hand over the pain and continues.

"Now I cannot even hope that a man's heart will change. With those things, it is just machine. No man inside. No heart, no God." Arman tries and fails not to cry as he asks: "What is my recourse? How can God expect me to pray? What kind of god gives a man a family that has no hope of protection?"

The angel feels a familiar pang of guilt. Long ago, when he had been a beloved member of creation, he had performed this very duty: consoling man with the lyrical, vague words God gave him. Humans would always ask their questions so plainly, so simply, but the answers he was allowed to give were lofty, purposefully unclear. They were meant only to guide, never to explain. Yet it had always hurt Harut a little, being a creature made from the brightest light, to occlude meaning. Now, though he is still essentially the same creature, made of the same stuff, he does not have any answers. It has been too long since he sat by, watching and worshiping, as God decided the way of things, dipped His fingers into the flow of the world. Harut does not know why things have come to be like this. When he stops to think about it, it shocks him too—though long ago he stopped believing their creator to be a merciful one.

"I have no answers." He doesn't bother to whisper.

Arman is surprised to hear such sadness in the voice. Are even the wicked, faithless spirits in the world wounded by God's ambivalence?

"Yes." The angel answers the question the man had only thought.

Arman nods, the jinni's solemn reticence more convincing than any answer. An idea of the world he has long held, but denied because it was heretical and wretched, is firming.

"Does any of your magic work against those manless things?"

"No," the angel whispers, anger and sadness in equal measure now.

Arman hesitates. If he cannot get explanations or protection, he does not know what he could possibly want from this cursed spirit. Yet still he hears himself asking:

"What can you tell me?"

The hope that swells in Harut as he speaks is almost equal to the joy he once felt when he sat close to God. "I can tell you how to leave. Remove yourself from this. Ascend to the heavens, though you will not enter the garden of Heaven. Settle among the stars. You will be on your own, separate from God and from creation."

Arman does not respond, and so Harut lets him sit with the thought awhile. The angel has developed, in the last thousand or so years, a humanlike understanding of privacy. Harut tries to focus his attention on the movement of the metal *thing*, the wind screaming as it tears through the dark high above, back toward the place where it does not rest, but is kept.

The sheep are baaing softly in their pen, and far away, farther than the previous explosion, another blast can barely be heard, sounding almost like thunder across the dry, flat valley land. The sound once made Arman joyful; rains were cleansing and life-giving. But the rains have slowed. Now all that ever falls from the empty sky is horror, and Arman holds his breath to better strain his hearing for a sign of where the *thing* has moved.

If God is beyond his forgiveness, Arman does not fear being beyond God's. His gaze settles on his home, filled with his sleeping family, and thinks of what it will mean to lose them, to be eternally lost to them. It brings fresh tears to his eyes, quickens his heartbeat. Yet the thought of leaving them the normal way—his dying, their dying, under those *things* so high and fast they cast no shadow—is unbearable.

Arman turns his gaze to the sky and feels, not for the first time, that it looks back at him.

"Would I have to watch Earth?"

"No, you can turn away."

Harut steadies himself, his hope. Though he still tries not to look, to spy too closely on the old man's considerations, he can feel it happening. It is so big a thing for a creature to decide to leave God—so unforgivable. The old man nods and in that same moment his heart, his soul, cracks. Overripe, over-ready.

The angel once again places his lips against the human's ear. That secret name of God, on angel's breath as on man's, is softer than a sigh.

SOMETHING
HUNTED

by ANANDA NAIMA GONZÁLEZ

DEAR DIANE,

I've had a long day and my voice is giving out and if I just keep the door closed, I think I'll be safe. Just keep the door closed, Diane. Just tell your friends you hate them. Be honest. Say, *Hey, this is not fun. This is not anything close to enjoyment. We're all simply white-knuckling our way through existence together.* If I called it quits today and sent off all my thank-you letters and apology notes and hid out behind my door, I think everything would turn out all right. Or have I been around too long to be forgotten forever? I mean it, Diane. If I just stayed behind this door and never went out or answered my phone again, do you think the world could really forget me? Could my existence be erased simply by hiding, or did I make too stellar of an impression the first time around? There are so many events I didn't even want to attend in the first place, but I hadn't yet accepted that I could live a life on the other side of the door. I had yet to look in the mirror and say, *It's your damn oyster. Close the shell walls and hide out in the damp dark. You've earned it, babe.* But now I reserve the right to leave whenever I want, however I want. So listen, Diane: I'm no star. I'm no attention whore. I never broke a bottle against the wall or cheated on my husband, for I have no husband. None of these details are important, Diane, and hopefully we'll get to the point where there are no points and we're on opposite sides of the same door. And maybe you slip your fingers under the crack and our fingertips touch, but, Diane, you know me. I'm not clever. I'm no prodigy. I'm something simple and faint and, if I'm lucky, wispy. I wash out in the breeze, for I have such a small face and such small feet that, really, you ought to forget me already.

I read something the other day about some boys who went hunting, and when they returned from the woods, the dad didn't see anything dead in their hands, so he assumed the hunt had been unsuccessful. But no, the writer wrote. Dad was wrong. Something had been hunted. And it was one of the boys' sense of self or something. And that line gutted me because I get it. That makes sense. I'm hunted. I can't even hide behind a door anymore. I'm floundering around back here. And soon I'll be found out. Soon they'll say, *Well, she was talentless and a liar. That was the extent of her charm.* And oh, how I've lied, Diane. I went on dates and should've kept my mouth shut when the men asked if I thought them handsome. But how do you say, *No, not at all. You ought to stop that, asking so shamelessly for compliments. What a vile little trait. Your parents ought to have beat it out of you when you were young. You insecure ape.* How do you even say that to someone's face, let alone someone who's just curious to figure out your opinion of them?

The other day I saw this film about a rural Spanish boy who grows into a giant and is dragged around the world like a circus act. The joke is that he can't speak the queen's Spanish, so not only is he huge; he's also dumb. The queen feels especially royal when the giant extends his arms to the side and she can walk under his limbs. She yells up to him, but he can't understand a thing. So, *ding, ding, ding,* round uno has just been won with no effort at all. And that's just the thing. I used to like a real fight. But now I'm happy to simply not understand what's being said to me. Disconnection is a blackout and busted lip of its own. I don't care anymore. I'm tired. I wish to close my eyes for a moment, Diane, if it doesn't bother you any. The incredible thing about this letter is that it won't be read. It won't even be sent. I'm looking for an exit strategy. And so, before I close the door, can you just look at me? Look at me and think for the final time, My god, she's divine. I should've told them all how divine she was. I'm trying to be like everyone else. Trying to feel entitled and grab at things that aren't mine, but I have weak hands and don't feel like bearing weight or eating more than my share.

Diane, do you think of that three-legged wolf when you see me? Is my beauty too dramatic? Do you think you deserve my attention? I don't care much about the answers. I'm just asking for a friend. My friend who cares very much about my soul, you see; she is a good woman; she was raised Christian; she is all the pleasant bits hovering about me, and I am tired of pushing forward as if this mattered. I went to the butcher this morning. I went straight up to the counter, Diane, and said, "The best cuts, the meatiest bits, right here, right now." The butcher took a cleaver to everything hanging in the shop. Ten chops through the air, and it was a mess. Hectic cuts of swine, goat, and calf falling to the floor. An ear here, a loin there. Brisket, flank, neck, and ass. He wrapped all the mixed-up parts of animal in brown paper, tied it with string, slapped it on the counter, and said, "On the house." I wish he were my husband, Diane. Just something about the go-for-it attitude. The swinging and heaving. The hairy forearms stained in sweat, blood, and the funk of salted meats. Whenever I think of him, I think of exposed bone, luxury knives, and legs dangling from the ceiling by hooks. At what point in my imaginary marriage to the butcher should I have said, *I'm a vegetarian, baby. I don't have the stomach for what you're putting out.* At what point do you look at the man you love and deny the totality of his existence? Luckily, the butcher works late nights and early mornings, so we don't share many meals. In fact, he's never seen me eat. Never seen my teeth, Diane. And despite it all, our life is actually quite extravagant, though the floors and towels are streaked with reds and pinks. But what man doesn't bring his work home constantly? We are very wealthy, Diane, and gaudy, and eager to annoy you with our riches, if you will allow it. What a dreadful imagination I possess.

We ought to all plant ourselves behind doors and forget one another, Diane. For the heartache caused by butchers, giants, and hunter boys is far too much to bear, if I'm being true. "This is it." That's what everyone keeps saying. And I can't tell if that means, *Things are so incredible and it can't get any better*, or *This is all that remains. This is all we have left. This right here. The crumbs that not even the rats are willing to eat.* This is it, Diane.

Yours Truly,
V.

TROUBLE

by TIMOTHY MOORE

JENNY LING IS CAUSING trouble again. Jenny Ling is asking the tough questions. Jenny Ling wants to know why women can't participate in Gādoman. The men say, "It is the sacred responsibility of young men to safeguard the Tacoma Peace Center and the members within," but Jenny isn't satisfied. It's not that she has secret dreams of moonlighting as a security guard; it's the principle. If this is the century of women, like all her leaders say, and if they believe, *truly believe*, that women will lead the world in the Buddhist millennium to come, why can't these very same women protect their fellow bodhisattvas?

The Men's Group hawks are irate and try to condescend Jenny Ling away: their mistake. When she raises her hand during guidance, they can't brush her off with the flowery metaphors they use to placate most youth. Such methods insult her. She's a college grad, poli-sci, two years out. She believes symbolism to be the root of banality; her faith is concrete; her thought process is stuck on critical. One thing that everyone should know, above anything else, is that you categorically, in no way, ever, want to get Jenny Ling angry.

In college, Jenny fought with Residential Life to get coed dorm rooms implemented by her sophomore year. Then, coed bathrooms throughout the campus. At her summer receptionist job for the anti-nuclear nonprofit Bombs Away!, Jenny shamed the assistant director, who had called her "babe" so ceaselessly that he had to apologize to her both in a handwritten letter and in front of his entire bemused staff. And then Jenny quit the next day.

Old pioneer members whisper that Jenny is too pretty to be so angry. She doesn't smile often, and she almost never laughs, and that's troubling for the members, who depend on their young women to bring cheer and encouragement in times of need. Even more troubling is hearing from the Young Men's Group leaders that Jenny has been radicalizing the young women since her return to Tacoma. That she's turning them against the young men by identifying them as oppressors. Brandon Hu, a few years out of college himself, says that Jenny Ling is a vessel of Sansho Shima—an obstacle arising from fundamental darkness. He's been trying to ask her out all year, including one drunken night in the parking lot behind El Toro's, one of the few times Jenny accompanied the Youth Group leaders for a drink. Brandon had sloppily pressed his hand on her right shoulder as he walked Jenny (unprompted) to her car, and then just stood there by her car door, whispering in slurred words that she was so much prettier like this, under the moon, the stars, where they weren't, for once, arguing about Buddhism—a moment that later he would not admit had occurred, not to the other young men whom he repeatedly told that Jenny had tried to kiss him. Those young men had scoffed at the thought of meeting tongues with this strange, angry girl but were secretly envious of this salacious affection. In truth, Jenny had pushed Brandon's head away and told him to get a cab home, take an Advil, and chant "Nam-myoho-renge-kyo" until he grew up or passed out, whichever came first.

Jenny, she has been chanting five hours a day ever since she came back to Tacoma a year ago to stay with her parents, after not receiving the job offer she had counted on following her internship. When she's not on the computer sending out résumé after résumé for positions she knows she's overqualified for, she's in front of her parents' shrine, legs crossed, hands pressed together, chanting. Jenny chants for two hours in the morning, two hours in the afternoon, and one more hour in the dead of night, setting her alarm for 3:00 a.m.—most bars aren't even open then—to chant when the rest of the household and most of the county are either drunk or dreaming. The shrine is made of a glassy faux ivory that is painted black, and it has the size and shape of a small flat-screen television. Her high school friends joked that the shrine was a TV to the netherworlds, but Jenny never laughed when they said that. Instead, she would tell them the single Buddhist fable she enjoyed, the one about a Buddhist priest from over two thousand years ago, who, on a desolate road, meets a weakened demon who holds a secret sutra. This pitiful demon offers to teach the priest the sutra if he willingly gives the demon his warm flesh to eat, piece by gory piece.

Jenny doesn't have many friends. Not in Tacoma, not anywhere. Jenny likes people only in the smallest of doses; she'll like them and then grow tired of them and then she'll have to sleep half the day after seeing them just to regain the energy that they have drained from her. People think Jenny lacks patience, but they're wrong. They've seen her only at the point of exasperation. In reality she is almost always annoyed at people's pettiness, their small thinking, their ingrained stupidity, and they have no idea how much effort she wills on a daily basis to hold that irritation at bay. That's why she chants five hours a day: because she desperately wants to be at peace with every single person in this trying world.

It's difficult, so difficult.

Jenny ended up back at her parents' place because she has problems with networking. Because she refuses to procure and then use procured connections. Because the nonprofit world is smaller than you'd think. Because when she was cued to appease, she became indignant. She's grown accustomed to big cities like Chicago and New York and hates it here in Tacoma. She hates the whole state of Washington, even metropolitan Seattle. She hates that it rains just about every day but that the rain is never satisfying or spiritual in the way she imagines rain can be; it's a mild, inoffensive rainfall in a temperately amiable climate that is never too hot or too cold or too anything except infuriatingly middling. She'll walk in the rain and barely get wet. She'll stroll along Tacoma's waterfront and sit on the flat rocks and she'll want to breathe in Commencement Bay, but the smog from the paper factories always makes her throat itchy. Not itchy enough to cause pain, just itchy enough to annoy.

All the Men's Group leaders in Tacoma have a shared, recurring dream about Jenny Ling that none of them are aware of mutually harboring. Of course, they would never discuss these dreams with others, especially not with men who hold similarly esteemed leadership positions. They dream about Jenny Ling but their dreams are never of the illicit nature they would perhaps welcome; their dreams are more abstract, filling them with a terror that rushes into the tips of their fingers and causing their hands to shake lightly every time Jenny Ling so much as clears her throat. In their collective dream they are at the Tacoma Peace Center and they are at the podium and they, or someone they exist as in the dream, are speaking, but nothing they say makes any sense; it's just gibberish, and Jenny Ling is laughing, and they've never actually seen her laugh, but in the dream this laugh is low and voluminous, and it becomes a never-ending loop that they are powerless to stop.

Jenny Ling isn't satisfied. Jenny Ling tells Phil Monroe that what he's saying is patently false. She tells him that if the Buddha of the Latter Day of the Law were somehow here now, he would weep with unimaginable shame. Phil doesn't know quite how to respond to this hyperbole, so he says that if Jenny sees an error in the practice, the error must originate from within herself, because the practice is infallible.

Jenny tells him that the *organization* is not the *practice*. That *Phil Monroe* is not the practice. The other members at the group meeting squirm in their plastic deck chairs, the semicircle they have formed around Phil Monroe's Gohonzon shrine an unwilling audience to his humiliation. Jenny has noticed that overcompensating Buddhists do not buy audacious sports cars; they instead purchase extravagant altars. This shrine rises fourteen feet from the ground, so high that the top nearly hits the ceiling. Sanskrit and intricate wood etchings of doves and lotus flowers decorate the ornate doors; the inside is bright gold and houses the Gohonzon, a scroll of such immense power that to duplicate it by pencil or by photography is forbidden and ensures a hell of ten thousand sufferings.

The members have never seen Phil turn this shade of dark pink. His smile is fractured. The old Japanese women curled at the side of Phil's living room with their Gongyo books and beads on their laps whisper among themselves, "Jenny Ling is at it again. Always causing trouble." Jenny knows they are talking about her but her focus doesn't stray from the task at hand.

"Anyone of any gender should be allowed to perform Gādoman," she tells everyone. "Gender isn't real. This," she says, and she pinches the skin on her left arm, "*this* doesn't matter."

Phil's fingers shake. In his dream, they were not at his home; they were at the Peace Center, and then suddenly, at the edge of the world, on a narrow cliff, and he was talking but he was also tipping over the side. The effect in reality is the same. Phil is younger than most Men's Group leaders, who are usually in their early fifties to late sixties, but you wouldn't know by his weary demeanor and rigid conservatism. He'll talk earnestly about world peace and then will immediately bemoan pacifism in the Middle East, will encourage members to accept all people as they are but in the next breath will wish for the complete and total annihilation of ISIS, of the Chechen extremists, of North Korea, and that is where these old men stand: at the precipice of enormous hypocrisy. Retired vets and war hawks and patriots that just so happen to marry Asian women and come to believe in the reincarnation of their eternal souls.

Phil tells Jenny and the rest of the members that this is not the time or place to discuss issues of this magnitude, and the other members nod in agreement. Jenny is ignored when she says: "If not here, where? If not now, when?"

Not at the chapter meeting, where visiting Men's Territory leader Gary Williams tells Jenny that these decisions are made by those in higher standing than even him, far on the other side of the Pacific. Not at the Young Women's Conference in Olympia, where stoic Suzy Quill tells Jenny, first in private and then in front of the thirty young girls who once, briefly, looked up to Jenny, that they should focus on bringing in new members and not alienating the old. Not in the McDonald's drive-through, where Emily Lee, a decade younger than Jenny, fiddles with her iPhone in the backseat of Jenny's '98 Honda Civic, and tells Jenny that she's sick and tired of hearing about fucking Gādoman and asks her to just take her home already because she doesn't give a single solitary shit about anything Jenny has to say.

While Jenny's issue with Gādoman proves to be a breaking point with Buddhists young and old, it is inevitable that people have grown tired of Jenny's dissent. There is no sinister cabal constituted when people begin ignoring Jenny at meetings, when they no longer encourage her to attend. The members trust their young men to watch over them, to sit behind the front desk of the Peace Center, to come early and unlock the doors, to inspect the grounds for suspicious characters, to field calls, to stay late and wait while the old pioneers count earnings from contributions and bookstore sales. Why would Jenny Ling want to ruin one of the few constants in their uncertain lives?

And the young men? Many of the young men have left for bigger cities or for colleges out of state, or they have left the practice entirely, never to be seen again. Those who have stayed in Tacoma currently find themselves in the midst of a series of dead-end jobs and broken relationships. Gādoman is the single place where many of them can feel truly competent, and here's Jenny Ling trying to take even that away. Because Gādoman, to them, is sacred. There's training. There's an oath. Though they take single shifts in the afternoon, many times the young men will congregate at the desk together, three, four, some times five at a time. Together, they jockey for position by one-upping one another with humor that gets progressively more obscene; to be the most crass and volatile is what they seek, and eventually they'll give up on words altogether; they'll share screenshots of the girls they want to fuck and the girls they actually have fucked, quickly swiping those photos away at the sight of a pioneer or doe-eyed young girl, and then they will laugh hysterically and slap one another's backs, "*that was a close one*," but when the time comes, when the wooden striker hits the altar bell three times, the appointed Gādoman will close the Gohonzon shrine and will bow with respect, and there is pride, there is humility, they all feel it. When the Peace Center is closed, these same young men, these bodhisattvas, will congregate at dive bars up and down Pacific Avenue, and they'll drink until their sorrows take the shape of karmic destiny. Or until the bar closes and kicks them out.

And there is a place for young women to perform their tasks within the organization: Lotus Group. Before they refused to engage with Jenny, Young Men's Group leaders would quietly remind her of the delicate role she should embrace. "The place of a young woman is Lotus Group," these young men would insist. That is where young women master the art of patience and diligence, herding crowds into the Gohonzon Room, bringing tea to respected leaders. While Gādoman is there to protect the bodhisattvas, the role of the Lotus Group is to serve. Doesn't she understand? She has a place in the organization that is just as important as Gādoman, probably even more so.

Hearing this from the young men does not incite Jenny Ling's anger, as one would expect it would, from knowing her. When she listens to the young men at their most earnest, Jenny's heart breaks for them. When she's alone and exhausted, she chants for them still.

Even so, Jenny Ling finds herself adrift. Not even her parents talk about the practice in front of her. They are dedicated to the old ways, meek and docile, and while they found Jenny's audacity to be cute when she was younger, it is no longer amusing now that she has returned from college. They believe that if they don't say anything, Jenny will come to her senses. They tell her they don't want to discuss the practice with her. "Let us be, please," they say softly, offering her tea and rice cakes.

It is not surprising that Jenny is cast out. The organization, by design or by practice, can be untenable to the educated, the college-age young. It runs on the backs of the old and the adolescent. When they proclaim that the youth are essential, they are referring only to those who can be guided: the elementary student, the middle schooler, the devoted and amiable teen. And then, after years of denying the practice, the educated will return, having started their own families, ignoring the perceived injustices within the organization that made them leave the practice in the first place. They crave that normalcy, that familiarity, and no longer see themselves in the recent college graduates who seem overly smug in their fervor for social justice and accusations of patriarchy. But mostly, these returning Buddhists miss their parents. And so the old ways, they continue.

That fate will not befall Jenny Ling.

For now, at what can be described only as one of the lowest points of her life, Jenny Ling walks along the Tacoma waterfront alone. It's the afternoon, and small crowds of families and children meander on the rocky shore. Jenny doesn't think about them, or about her isolation, or even about the last phone interview she had, over a month ago, and how they haven't called her back. The interview had been cordial but guarded, as if the man interviewing her were being extra careful with the words he was using, and Jenny knew even then that they must have heard about her reputation and had interviewed her only out of morbid curiosity.

A little over a year ago, Jenny had thought her career was on track. She was interning at a literacy nonprofit, and had become close to her supervisor, a middle-aged woman named Sarah. Sarah seemed to respect Jenny, and told her many times how capable she was, more capable than many of the paid employees. She had even encouraged Jenny to participate in the office's weekly diversity meetings, and Jenny tried to go above and beyond, suggesting ways to make the office more accessible for people with disabilities, pointing out that the staff was mostly white and offering to help HR recruit more diverse employees.

But at the end of the internship, she wasn't offered a full-time position. Sarah called Jenny into her office to tell her the news, not meeting Jenny's eyes as she explained that a few staff members had expressed concerns about her interpersonal skills. At the time, Jenny couldn't believe it. She asked if her suggestions at the diversity meetings had offended someone. At that point, she wouldn't have taken the position if offered, but she needed to know.

Sarah shook her head. "This is just what I'm talking about," she said, clearly frustrated. "Sometimes," Sarah said, "you just have to let things be." And then, seemingly to calm Jenny, she offered to be a reference.

Jenny Ling certainly can believe now that everyone will always want her to let things *be*.

A droplet of rain lands on her sleeve, and she looks up to see dark clouds speeding toward her. Behind her, bikers twist between pedestrians, children scream obscenities. To her right, a restaurant is moving the patio seating inside, the waiters in a muted state of panic. A steady stream of parkgoers rushes past her toward the parking lot, intent on getting their young families to the safety of their dry suburban homes.

Jenny ignores them and stands out in the open. A few more drops hit Jenny's shirt, her jeans, her long black hair. A drop rolls down her forehead, even gets into her eyes. She imagines the rain coming down hard, slingshot from the sky just for her. She stretches her arms out and waits. But the drizzle dries up as suddenly as it started and within minutes the park is repopulated with parents who have unloaded their strollers and taken their kids back to the water. Typical Tacoma: always a threat, but never a storm.

Jenny knows that she will leave Washington, possibly forever, but can't, at that moment, foresee the means of her escape. She checks her phone to see if she has received a job offer in her spam folder by accident, but still there is nothing. She thinks about how she never told her friends the final part of the Buddhist fable. When the Buddhist priest decides to sacrifice his flesh to learn the secret sutra, the demon reveals that he is not a demon after all, but a mighty Buddhist deity. The priest not only receives the secret sutra, but also, as a reward for his intended sacrifice, lives a life of immeasurable fortune. Jenny Ling never shared this part; the ending had always felt like a cheat. The real lesson is there when you end the story early, when the priest stares into the demon's pitiful eyes and agrees to the terms. In that very moment, he accepts his fate. For surrendering to his beliefs, he will be completely devoured.

Modern Homes

by Gabrielle Bell

A Place of Your Own

Members get free shipping and save 10%

Cotton Tufted Love Seat, $1,099 NEW
Alpaca Wool Coverlet, $89.95
Cheval Polished Silver Side Table, $199
Smoky Gray Sipping Glass, $4.95
Heather Wreath, $49.95 NEW
Ordinary Linen Rug, $999
Blue Languor Tiles, $39 ea.

Appetite for Design

Center of Attention

More options, more attitude,
more ways to express yourself

Multicolored Woven Pillow, $119
Serenity Throw, $89 NEW
Jayhams Woven Lounge Chair, $599 ea.
Lidded Drum Table, $379 NEW
Legacy Fretwork Side Table, $699
Kiera Table Lamp, $439
Primordial Rug, $1,299 NEW

Kitchen Solutions

Members get free shipping and save 10%

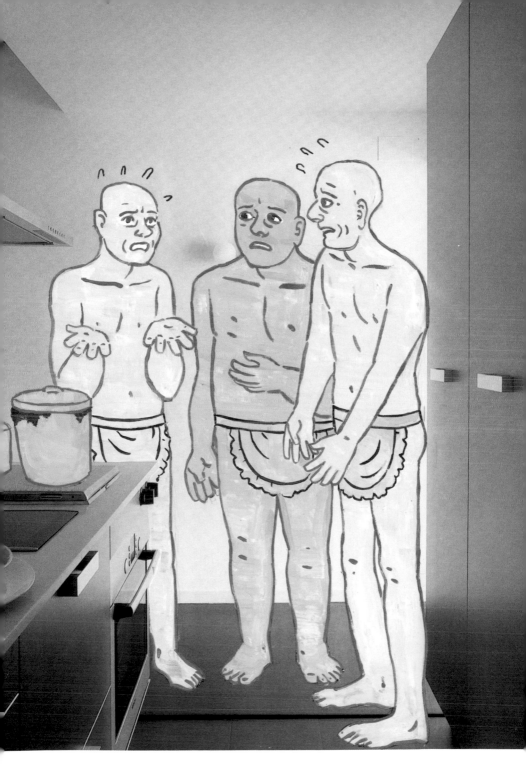

Handy problem-solvers
for the busy kitchen

Pine Monolith Dining Table, $2,999
Alabaster Serving Tray, $179 NEW
Green Glass Carafe, $59 NEW
Domed Ziggurat Chandelier, $149
Periwinkle Apron, $34.99 ea. NEW
Normal Porcelain Bowl, $29.95
Wineglasses, $14.95 ea.

New for Summer

Shelter-Arm Sofa, $1,999
Gray Afternoons Pillow, $84 NEW
Camden Wing Chair, $1,239
Broderick Coffee Table, $1,169
Broderick End Table, $849 NEW
Snell Display Bookcase, $1,699
Scooped Armchair, $999

Holiday Preview

Velvet Pod Club Chair, $999 ea. NEW
Reyes Olive Wood Coffee Table, $799
Marble Catchall, $99.95 NEW
Troy Metal Vase, $39.95
Paxton Saddle Leather Sofa, $2,599 NEW
Stippled Black 20" Square Pillow, $39.95 ea.
Brass Paperweight, $39.95

Relax
and Reset

Marble Slab Tub, $3,299 NEW
Loofah Bath Sponge, $14.95 ea.
L-Shaped Metal Faucet, $49.95 ea.

A Moment of Quiet

Simple Wood Bed Frame, $1,299
Tubular Marble Vase, $54.95
Striped Linen Blanket, $289.95
Goose-Down Pillows, $79 ea.
Striped Linen Pillowcase, $49 ea.
A-Neck Wall Lamp, $89 ea. NEW
Walnut Barrel Side Table, $99

Members get free shipping and save 10%

The Great Indoors

Polished Silver Dutch Oven, $479 NEW
Sawtooth Drying Rack, $39
10' Window Blinds, $99 ea.
Oblong Hourglass Decanter, $49 NEW
Brushed Silver Drawer Pulls, $29 ea.

Everyday
Inspiration

Round 22" Serving Platter, $49 NEW
Embroidered White Coverlet, $199
Down Pillow, $39 ea. NEW

A NON-SPRINKLERED BUILDING

by GERARDO HERRERA

THERE CAN BE NO illusions now, darling.

When you find your Saturday evening thrust into what can with any accuracy be described only as an *inferno*, there can be no illusions. When you have seen with your own eyes a chandelier ignite and disperse itself through a packed and clamorous room like a dandelion made of orange light, there can be no illusions. When you have—along with a crush of former revelers—circumnavigated a ninety-degree corner with the collective and unspoken expectation of an outwardly opening exit and thus salvation, only to be met with the dreadful sight of yet another stretch of hallway choked with a crowd that does not move forward despite a steadily descending ceiling of fumes, there can certainly be no illusions. And even though you are not with me—even though you dream safe and sound in the bed I tucked you into while Yvonne, your bedraggled minder, eats us out of house and home and really, truly believes I am not cognizant of her ungodly-houred telephone calls to someone indubitably male all the way up in Chautauqua—there are things *yes there are things* that must be laid bare so that there is no question. And even though you will not hear them, I will know them in my heart and so you will also know them in your own when tomorrow, in the gloom of almost-day, you blink away your sleep, and a man holding his hat in his hands, as custom requires, imbues you with an orphanhood that may at that fateful moment seem to be the end of all things but that will instead be where you summon the strength I know you have and prevail over whatever may come: perhaps your father will make his way home. I do not know where he is, is the thing. Said he'd left his wallet in the car. That leather monstrosity he makes a big show of producing whenever you and I ask for the slightest pittance. He held up a finger earlier and patted and repatted pockets he knew damn well he'd already checked while our waitress *hello my name is Josephine I will be your server for the evening* smiled distractedly at your father's idle jokes about not being able to wash dishes worth a damn and so I said *you're telling me* and there were laughs all around, including from the older couple Josephine had been kind enough to find us space next to despite our late appearance, and for a moment a good time—yes, I will admit it—a good time was had by all. Even by me, whom your father had just minutes previously accused of being a stick in the mud for remarking that the place did not resemble so much a nightclub as a *compound* where people are rounded up and entertained by force. But when it became apparent even to him that he did not have means of settlement on his person I said *Harold, but Harold, if it's anyplace it's on the nightstand where you always leave it when you change into your allegedly good pants because where else could it possibly be it is not—it is not, Harold—the sort of object that can simply be misplaced.* One does not simply misplace something of that magnitude. You know—you were the one, let us recall, who sidled up to me during that long weekend and dared me to disturb it from its recliner-side resting place under cover of snores and then measure its width against the only thing that turned out to be handy: the *A* volume of our creaky *Encyclopaedia Britannica* set, so old that Nixon's presidency terminates in an en dash instead of on the fifth floor of the *Washington Post*. The wallet's topmost bulge was exactly level with the entry for Antaeus son of Poseidon and of course that was our new nickname for the man until the day he overheard our giggles and demanded to be let in on the joke, which evaporated as soon as you tried to explain it to him *and but I said please don't go please don't leave me alone I'll pay for everything it's hot it's so hot why is it so hot in here* and your father could only look at me in that way of his where he all but says *hush* but actually says *let's at least have Yvonne earn what she's already taken from our refrigerator* and then off he went, excusing himself so many times to so many people that he at long last found it necessary to replace the permissionary *excuse me* with the exculpatory *sorry* for a fighting chance to reach the exit we were seated not fifteen yards from. As for me, I was left to stare with helplessness at the comedy stylings of Teter and McDonald, our evening's opener. I could have paid for the lousy food, I'll have you know. I have the means. I told him this repeatedly during his fruitless search; I have a job for crying out loud. Your father has never forgiven me for wresting the *sole* from his status as breadwinner. For insisting on doing my part to liquidate the mortgage I can only assume he thought would be paid by the brownies of Scottish folklore as he slept. The mortgage that has threatened to capsize this family ever since that Realtor's offer to show us something more "our speed" (after our tour of that magnificently renovated Queen Anne) got the better of his pride. As if I liked having to take the bus to the courthouse to transcribe the words of murderers, their obscene lies so carefully worded *find me innocent good members of the jury I am but a Kentuckian and a gentleman wrongly accused—my fingerprints have lives of their own*. Someone else's shorthand will be tasked with documenting what has happened here today I am afraid: *Occupancy limits in; number of exits (see also: widths of); state approval of blueprints and supplemental construction plans; locations of strategically placed fire-suppression equipment; inflammability of rugs and other decorative materials; who knew what and when*—and all of it will enter the public record, every last utterance immortalized in carbon copy from the opening statements to the defense's methodical portrayal of us as irrational collaborators in our formal-wear holocaust, given our abandonment of decorum in the face of wallpaper that cascaded upon us in giant sheets of flame; and how for example there was much laughter to be had at the waiter's expense after he scrambled onto the stage and strode toward our aforementioned comedy duo, placing himself between their repartee and staring out at the dead-silent crowd for so long and with such cartoonish fear that the unspoken consensus around me was that a joke must be forthcoming and that this joke would be hilarious, and but it was, everyone was laughing, only the joke did not appear to be a joke at all—*the building is on fire*—and even when the evening's entertainment shot each other looks of alarm and gently pushed the pockmarked and stage-fraught adolescent aside in order to stress to the assembled that this was no laughing matter, it remained one for a moment and then even for a moment after that before I at long last shot up and *thinking of you thinking always of you* slung my bag over my shoulder, suddenly arriving at the realization that the extreme temperatures were not, as the waitresses had claimed throughout the evening, a malfunction of the central heating system but in actuality the result of other parts of the building being incandescent with fire. And finally—as the record will show—the heat that had first manifested in menus used as fans culminated in the explosion of the back doors and the subsequent entrance of a dreadful entity of smoke that caused grown men in their finest to jump from table to table so as not to join the trampled and the petrified, the likes of which—and I'd raise my own hand here, dear, or would if it were not currently pinned underneath a hip that is not my own—could only stare through their sleeves at the surging throng accumulating at each of the inadequate and unmarked exits. I wish to state for the record that this was your father's idea, coming here. Me, I only wanted to watch *The Carol Burnett Show* and drift off to sleep in the middle of the *NBC Saturday Movie* but your father *oh your father* would not hear of such a thing, waving off my excuses and launching into a litany of the hardships he'd endured en route to the *attainment* of these reservations, which according to him was *no small feat, Gwendolyn.* Favors had been called in. *A man builds up a certain quantity of goodwill for moments such as these, people are at this very moment fighting tooth and nail to get a glimpse! A peek! John Davidson, one night only!* I had never heard the name but to me it sounded like it belonged to someone who might wander out into the audience and find a very special woman to sing to but according to your father, that shameless apologist for Captain & Tennille's maritime crimes against all that is decent and good, he was a very talented performer of the kind who ordinarily wouldn't be caught dead anywhere near here and aren't you always saying how you want to do something nice? Aren't you always saying that? My apprehension had a precedent. The entertainment your father chose was always something to be endured. You could only hope that it would be brief and that he'd elect not to break the silence on the drive home by asking your opinion of it. Disaster films and dinner theater. A performance of *The Crucible* in which the sound of chewing was as omnipresent as persecution. Poor Cotton Mather kept forgetting his lines, leaving those of us who knew Miller's play by heart to sulk in the lobby until Proctor swung. A Proctor, I must mention, that your father insisted should have talked. He fiddled with the wipers and insisted on this and when he would not drop the subject I was briefly inspired to quote John Proctor's concluding soliloquy, the one about how he has but one name and he'll never get another in his life, but I became frozen by the question of *whether I could utter those words without them stopping my heart.* Now, I am not going to lie here pressed inescapably into a filthy carpet by a sea of clawing bodies and claim myself exempt from the fantasy of the man who could be changed. Closeness abets all sorts of things but most especially illusion. You'd be surprised what you can come to believe with another's breath on your skin, someone who comes home to you and only you and whom you hold on to as if for dear life, this man of yours who whirls you around in a room with no furniture and no blinds and swears to you that he'd do anything. Am I to be blamed for misinterpreting this to mean that he'd look within himself and see there his limitations and in me the means to surmount them? But alas it turned out that he was a copywriter not just in profession but in his very soul—there was not a wonder in existence he could not tell to hurry up and get to the point. He found Ingmar Bergman not just dull but risible. *Wild Strawberries* was something he took personal offense at; he sighed so audibly during Victor Sjöström's rueful silences that he was asked to leave the theater. I found him scowling in the car nearly an hour later, shaking the ice in his soda like a rattlesnake, the weeklong silence he'd inflict on me already forming in his mind. The man hated poetry but loved limericks. Here is my own contribution to the canon, composed for just this occasion:

> Per the accountant's instruction
> Corners were cut on construction
> The place was a trap
> With nary a map
> To follow in case of destruction

But come to think of it, now that I recall my horror at your father's dinner party recitals, he only really liked *dirty* limericks. If you were with me here—and let's thank goodness *thank goodness* that I insisted this was no place for a child with an earache when Yvonne dawdled—and I told you these things while your father wandered out to the car, you'd undoubtedly pout and when asked what the matter was launch into your standard defense of your favored provider of horseyback rides, a defense that while making certain strategic concessions about his essential nature would still come down emphatically on the side of my being reductive and uncharitable in a way that said so much more about my own shortcomings than it ever did about his own, and what could your mother do in the face of those brown and blue eyes wide with hurt but stroke your palm and admit that you were perfectly right dear *of course of course you are dear* and gently remind you that you would not exist if I did not have at least a passing familiarity with his charms: uncommonly handsome, a smile like a swashbuckler in an early talkie, and just as brave. Foolishly and recklessly brave. Brave in a way that has me very worried about him right about now, the damned fool. Brave in a way that could not help but make the wild-eyed young woman he approached outside of that shuttered bus station feel entirely safe from the things she was running from, things she has not dared to tell a soul to this very day. *That bus you are waiting for will never arrive, I'm sorry to say it hasn't in years.* How I must have looked! Coatless and shivering in a southern cold snap that had caught me dreadfully unprepared. That filthy taupe dress I wore, torn and grass-stained. Your father has always insisted that the sight of me framed against that pale daybreak almost ran him off the road and that he backed up partly to make sure he had not been witness to something celestial. Note here, darling, that he makes his living from embellishments. I could not hear him over the sound of the wind, this man who had stopped his car. Who had rolled down the window to holler. My hair blew every which way; I wore it very long. He got out and I was afraid until I saw how he looked me in the eye—so many strange men I'd encountered. Dangerous men. They seemed to be everywhere I turned, uniform only in the way they leered at me, but he seemed harmless enough upon further examination, sheepishly offering me the coat from his own back and then searching his pockets for the car keys that the lopsidedly weighted coat itself still very much contained. *Mister*, I said. *Mister* and before I knew it he was watching me eat in the diner across the road, raising an eyebrow at my appetite and then again at the knife I produced from my own belongings and that I used to cut my cantaloupe. I kept it nice and sharp just in case. *Have you ever seen snow like this in Lexington?* is what he wanted to know. It was really coming down. The flat earth was met at the horizon by a sky with no color at all. This, outside of the window where we sat facing each other, the place deserted except for us. But the one thing—if you would have allowed me a rebuke—that I could never find it within myself to forgive above all of the injustices he would come to visit upon me was how he tried to seduce you with his lowered expectations. How he'd wrap you in his arms and dry your cheeks whenever I'd push you and expect the things you and I both damn well know you were capable of. How he drove five hours each way to collect you from the school that your mother, your very future at stake, moved heaven and earth to have you enrolled in despite—despite my informing him that I would never so much as speak to him again if he capitulated to those woeful telephone calls of yours, those shameful displays of self-pity, the sound of your tears billed to us collect from the pay phone outside your dormitory. I know. I know it was difficult being so far away from everything you've ever known. It was difficult for me, too, putting you on that train at Union Terminal. But who gave you the impression that anything worth attaining in this life does not require sacrifice? That the comforts of home could ever compare to the limitless joys of self-reliance? Identify this rogue—I wish to condemn him by name. And so yes, upon your ignoble return the task of your education fell to me. It was for me an unexpected blessing and the happiest I have ever been, imparting all that I knew. Seeing you there cross-legged. *Rapt.* The narrow aisles of the university library our sanctum. I know that at times my rigor caused you to despair and even to seek comfort in the aforementioned but it's just that I did not want the only person I have ever unconditionally loved mired in a mediocrity that is all too apparent in a place that outwardly admits to being a suburb of Cincinnati. Surrounded by those listless friends of yours who cling to your light like hideous moths. Kathys and Jennifers and Lilys—quintessential public school minds all: young adult novels about the attainment of boys clutched to their developing bosoms. Furrowing their collective brow at the screen door when I inform them that you cannot come out and play now and for the foreseeable future. Do they not understand that the only place for them in your future is in your wake? Really now, Mona, let us not pretend that you are unfamiliar with leaving your lessers behind. Have you forgotten your performance at the state spelling bee? Where you announced yourself to the world. Where you showed them what for, as my own father would have said—an advocate for victory if ever one existed. The poise with which you held forth! Your serene, unerring sense of supremacy in the face of that rapidly shrinking prepubescent mob that yearned so nakedly to take what was rightfully yours. Sweating and stalling for time that would only delay what had been a foregone conclusion as soon as I signed your name as present. They simply did not know what you were. *The tiny and inscrutable gears of your radiant mind.* I have told you, on the rare occasion when you have done something beneath you, that apologies are something base and—in a world where the present is all we will ever have and nothing can be undone—futile, but you should know that I bear certain regrets and I wish to take this opportunity to make them known to you. Firstly, Mommy is sorry about her melancholy episodes. Mommy is ashamed about letting you see her in such states, such endless and miserable weakness. Sobbing in rooms that were locked to you. Doors that you eventually ceased to knock on. Holed up in that bedroom under the covers, where I hid from the totality of my life. That cavalcade of daytime television the one thing keeping my mind from devouring itself whole. *Honey, these are the Days of Our Lives.* I found the endlessness comforting—nothing was ever resolved; those cardboard lives rearranged themselves perpetually in general hospital rooms with only three walls so that everyone could watch. I have seen the remains of the dinners you prepared and they have broken your doomed mother's heart. I'd break free from my misery to see macaroni and cheese that had not been boiled but seared. There it was: rock-hard pasta stuck to the pan, cheese powder poured upon it as if to put it out, and you—*oh you*—standing there next to the stove in your help-less ignorance as if it were your fault that you went unfed, cringing underneath the smoke alarm like some sort of kitchen island savage. Your teachers, they would call. Back when you attended public school, they would ring the house from their own homes sometimes, such was their concern. Dogs and husbands and their own children in the background, all of them with carefully considered words, knowing exactly how to couch the worries they had about the student who was already several years younger than her classmates. *Is everything okay at home?* is what they'd ask. Without fail. In those selfsame words. I never knew how to answer the question, is the thing. It was not a question. Not really. It was an invitation to confess something grotesque and lurid. Because what else could explain your state? I was not aware that they suspected malnourishment. That this was the verdict of that unpleasant school nurse who took possession of you whenever you were ill. I was unaware that they had someone come down in a government vehicle to interrogate you about *the fulfillment of my parental obligations*. I was further unaware that those other wretched and snot-nosed children *I wish upon them wasps* had made fun of your unwashed clothing. Your head lice. Some of the things that were asked of me were impossible, I am afraid. I would sit in that porcelain bath that was my refuge and the tasks arranged in front of me all seemed so terribly insurmountable. The simplest errands grew tendrils and fangs and terrorized me into a stasis I could not shake, submerged in that tepid water, and so you will have to forgive me if I let things pile up. The laundry. The dishes. The rancid milk in the icebox. The duties expected of a mother. Your father was forever away. It could not be helped, or so he claimed. *I go where I'm needed* is what he said to me while packing his ties, all puffed up with his newfound standing as the agency's golden boy called up to the big leagues. You need to understand. As if this were all that was necessary to explain his absence from yet another milestone in your life. You really should have seen him in airports. I mean really, really seen him. I did. The man was in his element. Consuming terminal coffee and gazing up at those infernal spinning departure times, he could not contain his glee: his face was almost unrecognizable with it. Perhaps it was because we would not be on those flights with him. Perhaps he was at his best because he was soon to be away from us. He was not as you know a fan of our mother-daughter enterprise. Our glances. Our raised eyebrows. Our silent judgment of his dinner table pronouncements. Oh, the pearls with which he'd grace us! (It is quite remarkable that we can both hold our laughter so well!) Our silent chewing was the only reply necessary. He was not privy. He couldn't be. He did not have my blood pumping through his veins. Neither had he inherited my complete heterochromia, those eyes of two different colors that will, I am giving you fair warning, forever draw attention when all you want to do is hide. Asked about his profession at social gatherings, he was fond of saying *I attach desire to objects* and indeed he did, specializing in detergent and favoring brute force whenever possible *hey, Gwennie, how does this sound to you: Soap Bully beats up stains*—subtlety his sworn enemy. He'd dump onto my lap advertisements that did not exclaim *BUY THIS!* and make me listen to his harangues about the decline of the form, the fall of the empire of *just coming out with it*. He'd been met with increasingly diminishing returns, and our fortunes had plunged. Bitter talk of a young new star—the mastermind, they called him. A bona fide member of Mensa, literally passing around the membership card to a previously incredulous table during a brainstorming session, and that's where I assume your father got it into his head that he'd join too. The afternoon that the results were mailed to the house was the only time he ever laid a hand on me. Says he saw a smirk. Of course he apologized profusely. Of course he did, darling. The man is not a monster. On the contrary. In his contrition he purchased for me a necklace as expensive as it was hideous, actually taking it as a compliment when I idly remarked that it resembled a prop from *Cleopatra*. Even tried to joke about it after. Called himself my Andy Capp. The scar he left on my eyelid the punch line. *One of these days, Alice.* Seeing me sprawled upon the kitchen floor with one of the only looks of surprise he's ever gotten from me must have emboldened him because it wasn't long before he began baiting me in polite company. *Kent State Kent State Kent State. Weren't you one of those people, Gwendolyn.* His sneer in full bloom now. Weren't you one of those people. As if this were the first time he'd brought it up in front of the people he called our friends, my tacit and continuing disapproval of *our mission over there*, as he called it between mouthfuls of breakfast meats, the sanctity of which—the war, not the bacon—could not and would not be questioned *not at my table.* Not even in the face of that fleeing napalmed child's anguish, the verisimilitude of which he took an addlepated delight in questioning, the son of bitch: *She doesn't look all that burned to me is what I'm trying to say, dear. I don't understand why you're getting so upset about this* but Saigon fell and then so did he, off the roof that he had been warned by well-meaning professionals against re-shingling himself, and afterward he sat in that ragged and other-forbidden sofa lounger of his with a stiff drink, nursing both his shattered fibula and the pride he had invested in the wholesale destruction of the Vietnamese people until the televised spectacle of it—the clambering multitudes at the embassy gate, the burning barrels of US currency, the *pop pop* of small arms being fired progressively closer—became unendurable. There are things in this life that I have never given another moment's thought to, but the conviction with which that man turned around and blamed me—me personally—for what Ed Bradley described on the *CBS Evening News* broadcast is not one of them. Nor are the blank gazes of his coven of sisters that soon after appeared on our doorstep to care for the convalescent and—more surreptitiously—*for you.* My usurpers boarded domestic flights upon hearing the horrific news of their beloved brother, he of the college education found facedown in the hibiscus bushes by a passerby. *My how they fussed over you both!* Feast after feast descending upon my kitchen in a tag team whirlwind, all for your benefit, second helpings thrust in your direction *eat, eat, you are nothing but skin and bones* the three of them looking at me sidelong like some perpetrator they sought to accuse. And lord it was not long until they did, wondering aloud why for the love of god I did not hear your father's cries for help, discovered as he was hoarse and going into shock. Just you try explaining to people who've never approved of you, not engaged or with child, *never ever*, that being dead asleep with the curtains drawn at three on a weekday afternoon is a survival instinct every bit as valid as swimming from a leviathan. The eldest lowered her voice in deference to your being in the next room and declared that he could have died, knowing full well that I was in no position to say anything in my defense, at least not in the wake of a dinner during which you—apropos of nothing—told our guests how in the days before their arrival you'd padded across the street in your pajamas and stolen leftovers from our neighbors as they floated in their pool *that's how hungry I was cross my heart.* While the eldest spoke you appeared behind her, standing in the archway to the kitchen, chewing ice in clothes that—I noticed for the first time—I had not bought for you; that made you appear so peculiar to me, you wearing a frock I had no memory of placing on the counter at the department store. The way you looked at me sitting there being censured in my own home as if you *felt shame for your poor mother* brought me so low that I could only look down at my own hands and swear to myself *enough.* And so, soon after, I voluntarily subjected myself to more interrogations, these by a series of mental health professionals with a predilection for referring me to their colleagues, the last of whom threw up his hands after nothing could shake me from my sorrow and firmly suggested that the only thing remaining for me was a treatment that I will spare you the details of, my darling, but which, when I underwent it, found me at the market afterward having forgotten why it was I was there in the first place, telling the clerk, who'd asked if I needed help after my and my empty shopping cart's third appearance, that I was reasonably sure we needed milk, but when he led me to it, feeling at once overcome by the need to look him in the eyes *god, he was probably fifteen* and to describe to him why it was that the hair on my temples had been shaved. Electricity is what cemented our dominion over the natural world—it did not surprise me at all that it'd be so miraculous! For the first time I could remember, the light of day was not something I sought shelter from. Everything seemed so different! Everything I touched with my fingertips sent shivers down my spine: The grasses in the wild fields down the road. Linens pulled taut. And lo!—you were even more different still. You were very much a young woman now with your own ideas about things. I'd like to think that I played some part in your preternatural self-sufficiency but of course one can never say for certain about such things. I knew you'd grown apart from me. Perhaps it'd done you some good. But you should not have been so cold. You should not have called me by my first name. You especially should not have continued doing so for nearly a year before I begged you not to, before I found it necessary to get down on my knees at that Eskimo-themed ice cream parlor that once brought you such joy and plead for just a *Mother* even if just a frigid and resentful one. We were escorted out—birthday girl or not—but I carry with me no shame: *I thank you for your compliance, dear.* This era of our relationship is not one I like to recall. Your forgiveness seemed like something inconceivable. Of course I understood. I was put on sedatives but I understood. I cut off all my hair but I understood. I stood in the shorn and unfamiliar reflection of the bathroom mirror and wondered if you were some witch that had placed me under your spell, I loved you so much. And I ask you now: *Are you? Are you? You can tell me anything.* You do not have to feel guilty about your misfortuned mother's feelings. I was a rebellious young woman as well. My parents wanted to have me lobotomized. No, this is not entirely true. My father is the one who wanted to have me lobotomized. My mother's role in the conspiracy against my fourteen-year-old prefrontal cortex was one of no fuss raised, least resistant path taken—the passive atrocity of the foregone conclusion. It was just something she added to the long list of things she was powerless to stop. Like the grub worms that ransacked her garden and the gradual encroachment on her Mary Kay sales territory. I suppose it all began with the letter I wrote to *Foreign Affairs*. It was in response to an article my father had written[1] about the situation that had unfolded in Beirut over the summer. The article was a big deal, I recall: dozens of pages in length and given top billing on the cover. It garnered a great deal of positive attention and was considered a return to form for a man who had not published in several years. I specifically recall someone clapping him on the back and uttering the word *unassailable* in reference to it. Someone big and important. One of his more influential colleagues at the university where he was tenured. My father had stared straight ahead, beaming, the drink in his hand swishing from the contact. That is something I remember quite well. That crimson wave of brandy and my father's sly smile. I simply responded. I composed a letter on my typewriter, refuting his points one by one. It was a good letter, its arguments salient. All of it backed by footnotes from the man's own library. He'd given me a key to it after years of asking. After years of peeking inside. Those towering shelves and the oaken stepladder that I could hear creak even with the doors closed. He presented it to me as a gift after our dog Harrison was struck by a car and I was inconsolable. That key I used and treasured so much that I took to wearing it around my neck on a necklace despite my sisters' taunts. *Bookhead bookhead key on a chain. / Face all soggy after it rains.* My father was not amused by my editorial response, no. He was apoplectic, as matter of fact. *Incoherent with rage.* Literally

---

1. Alistair Ezekiel Fitzgerald, "A Blue Bat against the Moslem Horde," *Foreign Affairs,* fall 1958, p. 33.

incoherent. Sentences came out of his mouth that did not parse. This was in the car after he barged into Mrs. Bohannon's home economics classroom in search of me. I looked up from my lock stitch and was so startled by him standing there scanning the rows of running sewing machines that the window valance I was making became mangled in the needle. His eyes swept right past me and in the split second before they focused on what it was they sought, it occurred to me why it was he was there—the new issue! It must have arrived today; the month had ended over the weekend. They must have printed my letter! They must have! He stormed down my row and one by one the Singers fell silent in the presence of the intruder I had summoned with my insubordination, his trailing overcoat completely at odds with that pink and frilly room. Without saying a word he lifted me up by the arm and for a moment—just for a moment—I thought I could save myself by grabbing hold of the material that had bunched up around my machine, but I must have underestimated his fury because Mrs. Bohannon emerged from the supply closet to the crash of my overturned sewing table and the scattered shrieks of the girls who had moments ago been hard at work *what in heaven's.* My father did not even slow his stride as he pulled me from the room, declaring this a family matter that was not her concern. I took one final look at the faces of my shocked classmates—a parent in the school was always cause for discussion but this *but this*—and immediately began to plan an argument inside of my mind that began with my stating that I had not responded as his daughter but rather as a regular reader with a subscription of my own and as someone who was disappointed to see the magazine used as a vehicle for such hubris. Such imperialist nonsense. "Kipling's Vicarious Escape from the Dustbin of History," I'd titled my broadside, and this they had dutifully reproduced, but what really drew my father's ire was the editorial decision to *also* reproduce my grade—eighth—as well as the name of my school underneath my byline, and between bouts of his yelling I kept trying to explain to him that I had certainly had nothing to do with this but I could not get a word in edgewise. *Unmitigated gall* he kept screaming. The unmitigated gall. I will admit that a few of my rhetorical flourishes may have been unduly harsh. Perhaps saying that the main thrust of his argument— which was not inelegantly constructed, really, merely undeniably false—was "not so much begging the question as pleading for it on all fours and then asking for a raincheck when it is not available" was uncalled for, but surely even this could not justify the campaign of terror he waged against what was only just a child after he wrested the gunmetal key from around my neck and pointed at the heavy twin doors I was thereafter forbidden—*forbidden!*—to enter, *to even be seen near*! My exile from what I would've told you then was paradise had you promised not to make fun was not nearly sufficient, oh no, not for such a public slight against his precious reputation. He burst into the room where I was hiding from him to accuse me of being put up to my response by persons he would not name *you know who I mean, you know goddamned well* and, when I would not entertain such a curious notion, forcefully confiscating my cherished Voss Deluxe before it could type another word against him, subsequently refusing all inquiries into its whereabouts, even ones forwarded through my mother when it became apparent that I was persona non grata. This ugly episode escalated to the point of him not visiting my bedside in the hospital when my appendix painfully burst during the long drive back from a recital that he also did not attend, going as far as to reserve a seat so that when I looked out from the stage it would remain an empty space both next to my clapping mother and in my adolescent heart. In any case my mother *do not call her Grandmother because she is not she is a stranger, she is dead to me, and if she is alive that is a technicality and something that does not concern you do not go looking for that traitorous woman do you hear me* did her best to cover for the man, always an expert and scholarly translator of what he actually meant, filling the catastrophic silences that he routinely left in his wake with such deathless aphorisms as *you pay him no mind* and *they are only words* as if these were koans that would acquire truth with repetition but I said *Mother but Mother you do not understand, words they are everything, we are but their imperfect and decomposing vessels*. In August's twilight my sisters kissed me adieu and boarded trains to finer prep schools on the East Coast, abandoning me for roommates named Hadley and Sarah. There were to be no witnesses for what was to come. I ate dinner at a table with my betrayers without an inkling. Sitting against the oak in the front yard, I leafed through summer reading that was less required than I could ever have imagined. My mother looked out at me from the veranda; when I looked up again she was gone. Forces aligned against me plotting my oblivion, and I was oblivious—until I was struck by a divine warning. You may think your mother is crazed, but it is the truth. It came to me in a dream. In the dream I was watching the television with the volume turned all the way down, as I liked to do when I felt lonesome, which was most always. The sun was on the other side of the house and while looking down at my hands folded on my lap I became aware of a harsh shadow slowly stretching toward me. I looked up and it was my father. He had been watching me watching the television and from the way he stood there I knew he had been watching me for a very long time. This had actually happened. I had dreamed something that had actually occurred, a kind of divination in reverse. I experienced as a nightmare something I had let pass without comment in my waking life. Something in my father's expression had been underlined emphatically in the incident's nocturnal recurrence. The look on his face was what woke me. I was petrified; my heart was nearly pounding out of my chest, I was so afraid. And it was at that moment—my feet dangling over the side of the bed—that it occurred to me that I needed to gather intelligence. That something was very wrong. I gave the means of my reconnaissance a name: Monsieur Secret Téléphone. He was ivory and golden and heavy as a brick and possessed a sharp edge inside of his dial that years before had resulted in a shriek and a bandaged finger and was thus put away as Mother never wanted to see it again *never ever it left a scar it will be there forever I am disfigured look, look at it I will have a lifelong reminder of that infernal telephone* but I rescued him, pulling down the ceiling's trapdoor and desperately rooting around in the pitch-black with spiderwebs stretching all around me until I unburied my salvation from underneath a stockpile of ancient *National Geographic*s, wiping from his base calcified insects that blew away like dust, and ever so carefully unscrewing his ear, for even a sigh, *a breath*, could give us away *you are not safe you are not safe now or ever again* and in between my mother's endless thirst for the sordid gossip of that miserable tree-infested town of my youth—birthplace of Hemingway, home of wide lawns and narrow minds, as he himself called it—my father's voice lurked like a maleficent Serengeti predator that I had inadvertently backed into a corner with my treatise and then with my boundless curiosity talking, talking, always talking, pontificating endlessly to colleagues, engaging in circular arguments with his long-suffering editor that were small masterpieces of passive aggression, expelling air from his nostrils as if he could not be bothered with the lapses in his own judgment, lapses that had shown themselves with ever-increasing frequency in his slow but surefooted journey from scholar to crackpot. Dearest Mona, light of my life, I submit to you that the scariest thing in the world is not as you claim the black caiman that you believe against all evidence resides underneath the carpeting in your closet but this: crawling underneath a bed in a guest bedroom whose door you have locked behind you to ensure your non-discovery and plugging a telephone into a jack that you can only just reach by curving your arm around one of the posts to hear your father your own father, Mona, say something along the lines of *we feel that this is her only chance at being a functional and independent adult* and immediately knowing that he means you and that that sentence entails something so horrific *you don't know why but it does* that your first instinct is to hang up and go to sleep and pretend you never heard any such thing but you don't, no, you hold the earpiece so close to your ear that the entire left side of your face goes numb. And then out it comes, matter-of-factly: a surgical procedure, four-syllabled like Iscariot, one so unspeakable that you open your mouth to scream but are so terrorized that your mind has forgotten *how* and nothing comes out as you hear the details of your own crucifixion come over the wire, your father not even flinching, saying *fascinating, fascinating* as if he were hearing—dearest Mona—about the minuscule gradient of Rome's aqueducts. Everything was coming together now, your doomsday even took on a date, its noon scheduled for the final eradication of you, Eleanor Louise Fitzgerald, age fourteen, member of 4-H in good standing, winner of the 1956 Budding Scientist Award for your work in the field of humidity, specifically its effect on cricket populations, and then again the year following despite your sisters' invasion of your bedroom for the purposes of exterminating the wind scorpions that you went through considerable trouble to attain, and all because the princesses, as they were calling themselves in those days, came to the decision that those *things* were much too ugly and frightening to share a roof with. They sorely underestimated the spiders' cunning and deadly speed, though, and *they all escaped*, all five of them, fully grown and desert-armored, incensed at the thought of two soft-skinned nine-year-olds in tiaras and Mary Janes trying to kill them with rolled-up issues of *Highlights for Children*. The things darted underneath dressers and into closets, doubtlessly vowing revenge as your sisters stood there shrieking like twin sirens amid the broken pieces of the climate-controlled tank that you had built yourself in preparation for their arrival, prompting your mother—your hysterical arachnophobe mother—to hire an exterminator, the very one who slew the Lake Theatre's infamous giant rat and flee the house with her children in tow, as it would be a cold day in you-know-where before she'd sleep there without them all accounted for, all forty legs, *every fang*, disregarding your protestations, your factual assertion, that they were—despite their frightening appearance and highly aggressive behavior (they feared nothing as far as you could tell)—relatively harmless and possessing no real venom to speak of *it's not like we're dealing with a houseful of black funnelwebs here, Mother, really there's no need for such a commotion.* In fact, the *relatively* in your yawned assurance succeeded only in making your mother pack her bag faster and chide you with more bitterness for not making scale models of the solar system like a normal child would, and you all retreated to a suite in the Hyatt Regency downtown (your father said it'd take a lot more than five Arabian spiders to chase him out of *his* house), where you stayed, eating tiny sandwiches and cinnamon French toast (this part you did not object to) until the exterminator was led up to your mother's exorbitant bunker. He was an elderly Puerto Rican gentleman, with a caricature of a rat about to be guillotined on his hat, who looked to you almost seafaring on account of his eye patch and limp (he'd fallen down your rickety basement stairs, it turned out). Your mother would not budge until she'd personally seen and heard this man swear up and down that he'd *searched that house of yours arriba hasta abajo* and *killed 'em all every last one, ma'am, stepped on three and sprayed the last one with a black widow poison ordered up special from the company catalog for just this occasion until it waved a teeny white flag and keeled over muerto underneath the dinette set* and you were so upset at the way he punctuated the murder of your beloved arthropods by snapping his overalls that you ran out into rush hour on Michigan Avenue in tears, not realizing, until the taxis stopped honking and the nice bellhop led you back onto the sidewalk and dried your face with his monogrammed handkerchief, that he'd killed only *four* and sure enough after performing a surreptitious search of the house that took nearly six days you finally found the poor thing after noticing the cat watching the litter from its box fly into the air of its own accord; you'd stared into its makeshift burrow and watched it come out, undoubtedly finding the beetles within ill-smelling and generally unfit for consumption, and you picked it up and mourned its missing leg, promising to take it to a place where the rocks were cool and dry and the prey endless but first you needed to observe its reaction to various stressors and perhaps even to some supersonic vibrations if you could get your hands on the equipment at this late hour. The quintet of judges were all amazed of course. Because how could they not be? Your countenance. Your skittering creature. Your cardboard maze carefully decorated to look like the one from the isle of Attic legend. Your findings on arachnid adaption and capacity for learning. And there you are in the September 3, 1957, edition of the *Oak Park Leaves*, standing there primly with your ribbon and an unconvincing smile frozen on your face because according to the reporter, who could not grasp the basic ideas behind your experiment no matter how many times you put them a different way, that's what little girls who win big prizes like this do: they smile from ear to ear and are subjected to interviews where they are all but patted on the head. But no—your sisters are off at school and you are alone under the bed. Alone in this house with the man who in but a few days' time plans to wake you from your sleep with an overnight bag already packed—*we mustn't be late, Eleanor*—and who plans not to take no for an answer and who will drag you out of that bed and into your vivisector's chambers if it comes to that, young woman. There will be no one that can help you. Your mother will not be there. She will be in Connecticut with a sister she has never been particularly close with, not to help her redecorate, as she will claim when she kisses you goodbye and hugs you a little too tightly for what will be only a weeklong absence, but because she knows. That will be the conclusion of the dial tone that will greet you when your father hangs up the phone. She will have washed her hands of you. She will have washed them as clean as the house she kept. *Mother, why have you forsaken me? I am a good girl. I have eaten my supper. I have put my toys away, see? I have apologized to Mr. Janoski for cutting his flowers. I only wished to make you happy on the day of your birthday.* Coming home when she can no longer hide from what she has allowed to occur, she will tire of feeling your eyes upon her as she dries the dishes and will find you a nice place to rock back and forth, perhaps wiping the spittle from your slackened chin, doing what she can to hide the ache in her treasonous heart from your vacant smile that will thenceforth stare out from a window not visible from the street and will indeed stare out from wherever it is you are put—be it a respectful distance from the guests who know better than to ask of you, or, finally ultimately inevitably, in a facility for people just like you, upstate perhaps or downstate, where they stuck Mrs. Lincoln after the recovering nation grew tired of her grief, the place crawling with all manner of loons and cripples and *those who will not stop touching you.* Those who will approach you at the window where you go to contemplate a world that will no longer be the thing itself but the echo of the thing and run palms over you that will be sticky with that morning's vile breakfast and that will make you want to excoriate the parts of yourself that will never again be clean with wire mesh pot scrubbers from your predawn kitchen duties, which you will have had access to until you try to do just that. And then the visits that you will neither look forward to nor won't look forward to will come to such a gradual end that you will simply not notice when the third Saturday of every month does not bring a nurse pulling you away from the semicircular confessional that you will witlessly inhabit the periphery of, and explaining to you with great and necessary patience that there are very kind people here who wish to see you, dear, the same folks who the time previous kept repeating that they loved you very, very much even though you did not feel one way or another about them. The ones who bought you soda—purple was your favorite—but then left rather suddenly after the girls who had accompanied them both started to cry, probably, you imagined, because they had no soda of their own, and the day will come *yes it will* when the glimpses of what you once were will mercifully cease to cohere inside what remains of your gouged-out brain until you will have always been this way and never anything other than the fair-haired and many-freckled girl who haunts the corridors of the northeast wing, humming to yourself as an apparition might: a forlorn and skeletal thing in a gown that the moonlight lends a glow to as you pull blankets over the effigy of pillows you've left to weather the hour's restless sleep in your stead, sneaking past darkened nurses' stations in search of what will no more be there than those foregone summers that could scarcely contain you—bounding through the park, arms intolerable with books—or the sundry birds you will call out to in stupefied dreams, every one, raven and swallow alike, looking out past you as if it were you *as if it were you* that did not exist and this notion, instead of dissipating upon waking, will stay with you in moments such as these, in flight from gruff voices who call you by a name you have not turned your head toward in ages, the sound of it—*E-lə-nər*—making you run faster, tracking the undone hem of your gown through the sublevel passageways you will descend into to ask your mother to bring you hot chocolate and sing you to sleep but you will find nothing in that almost-darkness except a mattress caked in menstrual gore, the thing standing up lengthwise in your direct path like a slaughtered creature, rectangular in musculature and so horrible even in death that you will fall backward, aghast, into the roughshod custody of your captors, who will vow to put you in a place from which you will never again escape, where you will be visited time and again by a shadow that will appear from underneath your locked door, its silent presence enough to back you up against the far wall and lo! After visits too numerous to count, over a span of time you will have no way of recording, the shadow, it will speak: *You insubordinate child. You have gotten into Father's things. Did you think I would not find out? I have awoken you—awoken you from your nightmare* and then will disappear once and for all, knowing that his unholy secret is safe and will remain forever so and that the contents of what you in your reckless curiosity happened to unearth will die with the rest of the unknown. And all of this will have stemmed from that blasted typewriter of yours *for the love of god we are in here* the subject of which you would not drop even when Mother crossed her heart and swore to you that she would personally replace it with her Mary Kay money once the whole matter of the published letter blew over. *Help us.* It just did not seem fair is all. Your coral Voss Deluxe. Polished each and every day to a sunlight shine. Having it taken— over a letter!—just seemed to you beyond the pale. You had to go looking for it, didn't you? The nervous energy the week before your recital needed an outlet, *well enough alone* something not in your lexicon, at least not when it came to your beloved typewriter. You simply could not believe the story your sisters solemnly told you, the one about a grown man dragging it into the garage and ritually destroying it. Of course they were telling the truth. Your sisters could never lie to you without a mischievous look in their eyes that they passed between them like a ball. Still you tossed and turned trying to think of where it could be: it had to be *somewhere.* And though the house where you spent your formative years was in no way modest you scoured it from top to bottom, checking every last place where it could have been hidden until one place—and only one place— remained: the library. The twin doors were kept firmly locked at all times and your father had snatched your means of entrance from your neck so violently that your sister later noticed you were bleeding from the nape. *Hold still let me look at it* she said grabbing your wrists. The local library however held no grudges and without comment lent you all it had on the subject of locksmithing and though gaining access was not quite trivial your newfound journeyman's knowledge of tumblers made it possible, after a bout of trial and error conducted while your parents were away at a function. You heard a faint tick and the doors separated inward at your touch, yielding to a void that swallowed you up without a sound. The lights you groped for in the darkness hesitated over the five rows of towering shelves and you were among them in a flash, scanning high and low for any sign of it—the drab olive case; a protruding carriage return—*something.* Only—only... no. It was nowhere—nowhere to be found in the last place it could possibly have been. You fought the tears that came to your eyes as you dragged the oaken stepladder you used to search the library's greater heights back to its starting location, finally, finally conceding what your sisters pulled you aside and confided in you: you had had a typewriter. Past tense. And you were about to close those doors behind you once and for all when the size and dimension of your father's reading desk drawer and/or your Voss Deluxe must have become distorted in your mind because—standing in the archway, your head lowered in defeat—you came to the perplexing conclusion that what you sought must have been contained within a space that could not for the love of God contain it, turning on the lights once more *why, why did you do this* and venturing back into that nightmarishly flickering library to ransack your father's desk. You knew—you knew!—that the drawer was kept locked, this knowledge gleaned from your absentminded joggling while immersed in this or that text, and yet you reached out and turned the handle on it regardless and when the handle would not turn, pulled on the drawer anyway just—one would have to assume—as a stymied flourish, as an emphasis however fruitless and not in any way expecting that this would be all that was necessary for the drawer to slide off its track and onto your bare foot so forcefully that everything became pain and only pain, your racing thoughts obliterated by hurt so profound you could taste it on your tongue. You unbit the sleeve that muzzled your cry and verified that your toes were unsevered and, after you wriggled life back into them, you tried desperately to reinsert a drawer that you should have known did not contain your typewriter, only page after page of your father's false starts—the follow-up to his acclaimed volume on the economics of the Roman Empire was not going well—but no matter how carefully you placed the fallen drawer onto the desk's metal rails it would not slide all the way in. Your father would notice this as soon as he hung his coat on the rack—he would know. Worse even, when you resigned yourself to hoping against hope that he wouldn't, you slid the drawer in as fast as it would go and as soon as you ruefully turned your back to it you heard it once again crash to the rug. You took a breath and hefted the brass lamp from the desk and shone its light into the drawer-less cavity. There was something back there, an obstacle keeping you from erasing your presence here. You ran your hand along the drawer's track until your fingertips touched it. You pulled it out and studied it in your palm: a circular metal cap painted a bright red. You shone the light again and saw the glimmer of a curiously hidden fixture attached to the desk's inner wall: a brass plate with a hollow circular button in its center the very size and shape of the red metal cap you held in your hand. The cap must have come loose when you'd inadvertently pulled the drawer out. You thought it absolutely vital to set the room exactly as you found it and so you stacked books on the floor and placed the lamp on them and with the light provided you took the curious metal cap and reached out as far as you could toward the rectangular plate, pressing the hollow button against it until you felt it snap firmly into place. And this was followed right then by another sound, one you immediately recalled hearing before—*yes that was it*—a sound you had heard less than intermittently at various points throughout your childhood, one that you were frightened of precisely because you so rarely heard it. You'd be underneath your covers on the cusp of sleep and a low rumble would come up from below your room—which was directly upstairs—only it was louder now and in response to what you had just done. Something had just changed—your actions had once more disturbed the configuration of your surroundings and for a moment the notion that the room possessed an invisible demon that would resist your every attempt to put things right again was present and not dismissed out of hand. You pulled your arm back with a start and rose to your feet with blood roaring in your ears from the quickening of your heart. The sound came to a stop and then started and stopped again and throughout this staccato sequence you propelled yourself toward it, toward a sound that was like something heavy and precarious being moved by clockwork and when you planted your feet at its origin here is what you found: that the only segment of shelf against the library's back wall—the one you'd always thought was curiously barren of books—had retreated past the very boundary of the room, revealing to you a set of shallow stairs that you incomprehensibly followed downward with what had to have been a last-ditch hope, the siren's call of all desperate hearts. And at the bottom of the staircase you came face to face with what was only for the briefest of moments the most sinister thing you'd ever come across: an entire hidden room, cement walled and subtly crooked and appearing in its unadorned blankness like a subterranean pocket that creation had known better than to disturb, the space utterly stark save for the cast iron lectern that sprouted from the dead center of the room in an anguish of broken masonry with what, it became apparent in your stricken and deliberate approach, was a book—now this was the most sinister thing you'd ever come across—resting on the lectern's slanted apogee, bound in carved lava rock and somehow heavier than anything of its dimensions could ever *possibly* be, the smell ancient, like something that had weathered centuries just to meet your touch. To say that your curiosity had gotten the better of you when you closed the door to the library with that very book in your hands would be putting it quite mildly indeed. It turned out in fact to introduce you to the concept of mortal danger at all of fourteen years. It was such an unusual object. Meticulous and baroque—an impossible amount of care put into every page. You marveled at it, carefully turning the pages, and swore that you'd return it as soon as you had plumbed its mysteries. Put it into some kind of context. However, apart from making an educated guess that the vaguely unsettling material used for the book's copious pages was likely uterine vellum, context would prove difficult to come by. Oh and if only the most unsettling thing about the book you held in your hands were that it was likely crafted from the flesh of unborn animals—*or worse*. If only that were the case. Because the book as a whole troubled you a great deal. A great, great deal. And the more you looked at it the more unnerved you became.

You cloistered yourself in the guest bedroom and stared. And when your mother demanded to know why you'd locked yourself in there—*what has gotten into you young lady*—you hauled it into the silent study rooms of your father's university and pored over its contents, shielding it defensively when the custodian came in to tell you that the library had closed forty minutes ago. You could not begin to comprehend it. It was written entirely in markings. Horizontal lines bisected every page—some of them straight, others arced to various degrees, each of them intersected by vertical red marks at intervals that could not be random but which resisted rhyme or reason, and these odd denotations hung like low clouds over painstaking drawings that did not leave you even when you shut your eyes against them. Images of decadent and promiscuous settlers in a faraway land driven mad by minuscule bugs. The sky darkening—an eclipse of the insectile. Page after page of colonists succumbing to a madness of itching; the elders at a loss. Details of the fingernails of the infested digging through their scalps until the blood spilled down their faces in columns and they were held down by hooded plague doctors and thrown behind doors bearing the markings of an insect silhouette. And this narrative was interrupted at other times by seemingly discordant elements: a levitating table and a priest who sought its counsel; congenital twins hip deep in a marsh; crops left to rot on the vine; a Victorian house plunging from the sky at terminal velocity—everything drawn flat in the manner of long ago; faces without expression, even when the insectile vectors of this peculiar epidemic overcame the hasty quarantine—crawling underneath doors and through every available crevice—and entire colonies were overrun by them, the flesh and blood that the insects fed upon apparently at their command. The volume ended with images of an apocalypse caused by hordes of the naked and the crazed who, yes, came to lay siege to civilization itself. Of unrestrained murder and copulation. Of legions of scalps scratched to the bone from itching. The eyes underneath them looked at something beyond—*and at you*. You slammed the book shut—your mother was yelling outside the door. You'd become so lost in it that you'd forgotten entirely about your dance recital and were caught so off guard by your mother's entrance—she had never entered without asking permission first— that you shoved the book into a drawer you neglected to close the whole way in order to whirl around and face her exasperation at you not being dressed yet, and the book remained there for days after your appendix catastrophically failed over the course of the evening. You doubled over in pain as the other girls gossiped and practiced their pirouettes, and later in your post-appendectomy hospital bed you cursed your wretched carelessness when you closed the get-well card from the other ballerinas, as that was the moment when it occurred to you where it was you'd last put it, and as soon as you got home—petrified that you'd left the accursed thing almost in plain sight—you took the first fucking opportunity to put it back on its lectern and tell yourself, as the false bookshelf made its way back into the library, that you'd forget about it if it was the last thing you ever did. But your father must have found you out. Yes indeed. He had stayed at home—you recall him glaring at your mother in his robe when she asked him if he was coming to the recital; she tearfully apologized for him in the car, dismissing your lingering stomachache as nerves. He'd often wander through the house in thought. One of his habits. He must have seen the overdue notice your mother had left on the upstairs hallway table outside of your room with the rest of your mail. A postcard from the library that must have been mailed while your head was in what you had found. *A Friendly Reminder!* it said, followed by the full titles of the quartet of locksmithing primers you'd checked out and neglected to return. The postcard wouldn't have been hard to notice. You eventually gave the chain of events a great deal of thought and this is what you surmised. That must have been all it took to rouse his suspicions enough to trespass into your room for a look around. Later you'd imagine him catching a glimpse of it in your drawer and stopping dead in his tracks. He must have seen it. You know he did. In your divine dream you realized that he knew. That is what his face said. He knew something so secret that he couldn't even accuse you of it, so while the surgeons were removing a useless portion of your body, your father founded a plan to mutilate a much more vital one as well. Only it did not happen. You can thank Monsieur Secret Téléphone for that. No. I pulled his cord from the wall and waited for the house to fall silent. I took nearly two hundred dollars in small bills from my mother's Mary Kay suitcase and with the crickets singing from an open window nearby I surrendered to an impulse—why, I will never know —to dump that infernal tome into my knapsack just before I pushed open the front door in the dead of night when not even my insomniac father stirred and I ran. I ran and ran. I ran for my life, my darling. I slept in a field of wet foxtails under the shadow of a departing thunderstorm and got up and started running again not five seconds after waking. The sun shone as if on me— the feeling like nothing before or since. I ran in light and in darkness and what was not quite either and the sorrow of never seeing my mother or my sisters again came to me mid-stride and I thought I'd stop but the wind at my back bade me onward! All familiar things ceded and in a town where wild dogs trotted alongside me and the factory gates were chained I boarded a morning train and the window I placed my hands on made the distance I spanned beautiful. I fell asleep with my arms around everything I owned and I was prodded awake by a conductor who asked me where my parents were and by the time I'd finished talking he apologized profusely for having bothered me—I did this so many times I lost count. I walked through a patriotic parade of the crippled and the maimed and as the trumpets faded I disposed of my clothes and put on others. Underneath a highway overpass I traded a sandwich I'd bought from a truck stop for a balisong. An old man in a filthy coat said it cut good and that he did not have any need for it because as far as he knew all of his enemies were dead but *I can tell from looking at you that you are not nearly as fortunate young miss.* We gave up yelling over the sirens and looked out at the tornado forming on the horizon. I would rip my own throat out if they ever caught up to me. I would do it with joy in my heart. I practiced this while trudging through weeds on the shoulders of interstates and waiting for fetid water to boil, tickling what I was sure was my jugular with the blade. I carved taunts for my pursuers on picnic tables and in the toilet stalls of roadside diners where the coffee kept coming whether you wanted it to or not. ELEANOR REMAINS UNGOUGED! ELEANOR REMAINS UNGOUGED! ELEANOR REMAINS UNGOUGED! I carved this over and over again, child. Go and see for yourself. I left my mark all along Route 31. ELEANOR REMAINS UNGOUGED! I rented a room from a taciturn spinster who asked no questions. *As long as you got money I don't care who you are* she said, interrupting the story I'd rehearsed. I worked. I washed clothes for the Salvation Army. The clothes spun round and round. I would not be touched. They would never catch me. In the pocket of a moth-eaten tuxedo I was told to throw away I found a photograph of a posed dead child and kept it. A tiny girl in a dark-collared dress stared out with lifeless eyes. This girl had a name I would eventually give to you, my love: *Mona—1901—consumption.* She was consumed. Consumed as this Beverly Hills Supper Club will be. In a moment of weakness I called home and could not bring myself to say anything. I held my breath and listened to my mother wail my name into the silence. *You come home* she said. *We are tracing the call young woman you come home this instant. If you will not listen to reason listen to your mother's tears. Listen to your mother cry over the telephone. It is three in the morning. You have undone us. You have undone us* and then there was a violent commotion on the other end and all of a sudden I felt my father's presence and immediately hung up more frightened than I'd ever imagined I'd be. Stupid. I saw the seasons change and smiled when the clerk at the general store wished me a Merry Christmas. I saw my own face tacked to the wall in a post office and I lingered there for longer than I should have. LAST SEEN the poster said. *I think I hear sirens.* The clothes it described had been tossed into a dumpster behind a Piggly Wiggly. And when a puffy-faced man in a brown hatchback called me by my real name outside of the house I was staying in I nonchalantly went inside as if the name meant nothing and reclaimed what little I owned and was forced to shove the woman who had betrayed me from the back door that she blocked and fled into the hills that sloped up from her wild back stoop. *The smell of burning hair is something that truly cannot be put into words.* And in the time that followed, both hunger and cold were my companions. I marched through wilderness and ate things I don't care to recount. I existed with hope and without, and shivered through storms with my only comfort being the knowledge that they could not last forever. I ran and ran. I ran into the arms of a man who asked me if I was lost and who honestly told me that I did not look at all like a Gwendolyn. I ran into the arms of a man who wanted to know preciously little and who was sorry that my folks had died under such tragic circumstances and who understood when I told him I did not like talking about them all that much. I ran into the arms of a man who gave me a little girl that I loved with every fiber of my being. They never found me. *Yes, I hear sirens.* They still have not. I will die in here never having been found. I will be engulfed by the fire that I have clawed my way to the very top of this tuxedo pyre just to meet, thinking it the light from outside. *Oh.* There will be no trace of me except for you and that infernal book in the locked armoire upstairs. Never let it fall into the wrong hands! Never ever! Do not tell them where I've gone child do not tell them a thing

AMANDA AJAMFAR lives in New York. Her stories have appeared or are forthcoming in *Colorado Review*, *Paper Darts*, the *Georgia Review*, and the *Southern Review*.

MARIA ANDERSON's fiction has appeared or is forthcoming in the *Sewanee Review*, *Alpinist*, the *Iowa Review*, the *Missouri Review*, and *The Best American Short Stories 2018*. She has been awarded residencies from Jentel, the Helene Wurlitzer Foundation of New Mexico, Joshua Tree National Park, and the Crosshatch Center for Art and Ecology. She lives in Bozeman, Montana.

MARIA BAMFORD's comedy special, *Weakness Is the Brand*, is now available on Amazon Prime for 99¢! You can find her at mariabamford.com.

GABRIELLE BELL's work has been selected for the 2007, 2009, 2010, and 2011 *Best American Comics* and *An Anthology of Graphic Fiction*. She has contributed to the *New Yorker*, the *Paris Review*, *McSweeney's*, the *Believer*, and *Vice* magazine. The title story of Bell's book *Cecil and Jordan in New York* has been adapted for the film anthology *Tokyo!* by Michel Gondry. Her first full-length graphic memoir, *Everything Is Flammable*, was named one of the best graphic novels of 2017 by *Entertainment Weekly*, *Paste* magazine, and *Publishers Weekly*. Her most recent book, *Inappropriate*, is a collection of humorous and weird short comics, usually involving animals. She lives in Brooklyn.

JULIA DIXON EVANS is the author of the novel *How to Set Yourself on Fire*. She lives in San Diego.

MELISSA FEBOS is the author of *Whip Smart: The True Story of a Secret Life*; *Abandon Me: Memoirs*; and *Girlhood*, which is forthcoming from Bloomsbury in 2021. Her essays have recently appeared in the *Believer*, the *Sewanee Review*, and the *New York Times*. She is an associate professor at the University of Iowa, where she teaches in the Nonfiction Writing Program.

LEAH HAMPTON is the author of the short-story collection *F*ckface*. Her work has appeared in *storySouth*, *Ecotone*, *Electric Literature*, and elsewhere. A graduate of the Michener Center for Writers, she lives in the Blue Ridge Mountains and writes about monsters.

GERARDO HERRERA is a writer in Iowa City, Iowa. He is working on a novel, *I! Am! Bernadette!*, from which the story in this issue is an excerpt.

BRANDON HOBSON is the author, most recently, of *Where the Dead Sit Talking*, which was a finalist for the National Book Award and the winner of the 2018 Reading the West Book Award in Fiction. His new novel, *The Removed*, will be out in early 2021 from Ecco. His fiction has won a Pushcart Prize and has appeared in *Conjunctions*, *NOON*, *American Short Fiction*, and many other places. Hobson is an assistant professor of creative writing at New Mexico State University and also teaches in the low-residency MFA program at the Institute of American Indian Arts, in Santa Fe, New Mexico. He is an enrolled member of the Cherokee Nation of Oklahoma.

JON MCNAUGHT is a cartoonist, illustrator, and printmaker living in London. His latest comic book, *Kingdom*, was released by Nobrow in 2019.

TIMOTHY MOORE is a writer and instructor living in Chicago. His work has been published in *Ghost Ocean*, *Oyez Review*, *Entropy*, and the *Chicago Reader*, among other publications, and he is a Kundiman and Luminarts Fellow. He is the recipient of a Hinge Arts Residency and earned his MFA from Roosevelt University.

ISMAIL MUHAMMAD is the criticism editor of the *Believer*. His work has appeared in the *New York Times*, the *Nation*, and elsewhere.

ANANDA NAIMA GONZÁLEZ is a writer residing in Harlem, New York. She earned a BA and an MFA from Columbia University, in poetry and fiction, respectively, and is currently at work on a collection of short stories. Her work is finely tuned to the tender and brutal realities of humanity, feral and natural energies, dreamscapes, and the inherently sacred ritual of living.

SALVADOR PLASCENCIA is an assistant professor of creative writing at Harvey Mudd College. He is the author of *The People of Paper*.

INGRID ROJAS CONTRERAS was born and raised in Bogotá, Colombia. Her first novel, *Fruit of the Drunken Tree*, won the Silver Medal in First Fiction from the California Book Awards. She is working on a memoir about her grandfather, a curandero from Colombia, who, it is said, had the power to move clouds.

SAMUEL RUTTER is a writer and translator from Melbourne, Australia. His work has been featured in *Harper's Magazine*, the *White Review*, *T Magazine*, and the *Paris Review*'s the *Daily*.

MELISSA SCHRIEK is a Dutch photographer who studied documentary photography at Royal Academy of Art in the Netherlands. Over the last year she has worked on several projects, including *The City Is a Choreography* and *ODE: An Exploration of the Dynamics of Female Friendship*. Schriek explores relationships between individuals and their environment through both observation and staging. Her work is often created with a performative approach, aesthetically and conceptually exploring the border between staged and documentary photography. With her sensibility for the body as a sculpture, she aims to create images that challenge our perception of human connection.

KIRSTEN SUNDBERG LUNSTRUM is the author of three collections of short fiction, most recently *What We Do With the Wreckage*, which won the 2017 Flannery O'Connor Award for Short Fiction and was published by UGA Press in 2018. Her fiction has received a PEN/O. Henry Prize and has been published in *Ploughshares*, *One Story*, *North American Review*, and elsewhere. She teaches high school English near Seattle.

HEBE UHART (1936–2018) was an Argentine writer and teacher who published more than twenty volumes of stories, novels, and articles throughout her lifetime. In 2017, she was awarded the Manuel Rojas Ibero-American Narrative Award. The five micro-tales included in this issue, translated from the Spanish by Sam Rutter, will appear in Archipelago Books' *Selected Stories of Hebe Uhart* in 2021.

SALLY WEN MAO is the author of the poetry collection *Oculus* (Graywolf Press, 2019), a finalist for the Los Angeles Times Book Prize, as well as *Mad Honey Symposium* (Alice James Books, 2014). She has received fellowships from the New York Public Library's Dorothy and Lewis B. Cullman Center for Scholars and Writers, the George Washington University, and Kundiman, among other places. Her work has won a Pushcart Prize and has been published in *Harper's Bazaar*, *Poetry* magazine, *Tin House*, *The Best American Poetry* series, the *Kenyon Review*, and other publications.

CHRISTINA WOOD MARTINEZ is a fiction writer whose short stories have appeared in *Granta*, *Virginia Quarterly Review*, the *Sewanee Review*, and other journals. Her story "The Astronaut" won the 2018 Shirley Jackson Award for short fiction. She is the editor of *echoverse*, a digital anthology of writing about the environment and climate change.

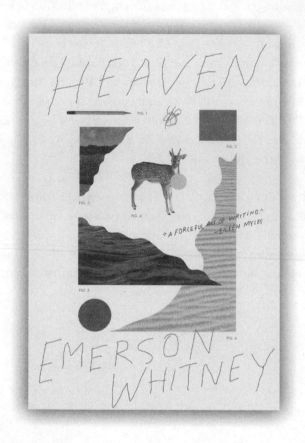

"*A poetic, candid, probing reckoning with childhood,
the maternal, gender, and the possibilities of theory, which
will both speak to its time and outlast it.*"
—Maggie Nelson

HEAVEN
by Emerson Whitney

An expansive examination of what makes us up, *Heaven* wonders what role
our childhood plays in who we are. Can we escape the discussion of causality?
Is the story of our body just ours? With extraordinary emotional force,
Whitney sways between theory and memory in order to explore these brazen
questions and write this unforgettable book.

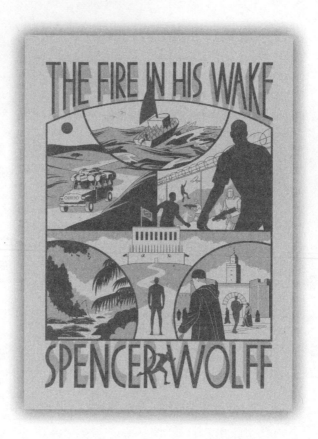

"*Spencer Wolff has done that brave and difficult thing we most need our novelists to do: painstakingly imagine himself into lives and circumstances starkly different than his own. It is an astonishing debut.*"
—Thomas Chatterton Williams, author of *Self-Portrait in Black and White*

THE FIRE IN HIS WAKE
by Spencer Wolff

The Fire in His Wake, Spencer Wolff's exuberant debut novel, tells the story of two men swept up in refugee crises of the twenty-first century: Simon, a young employee at the UNHCR in Morocco, and Arès, a Congolese locksmith left for dead in the wake of ethnic violence. When a storm gathers at the UNHCR, the two men find themselves on a collision course, setting the stage for the novel's unforgettable ending. Wolff brings his personal experiences as an aid worker to this unforgettable story of two remarkable individuals.

"Jaswinder Bolina's insightful, raw, and honest collection of brilliant essays illuminates the joys and pains of being a specific person Of Color and through his unique lens we also come to understand the universal ongoing story of America."
—Wajahat Ali, contributor to CNN and the *New York Times*

OF COLOR
by Jaswinder Bolina

In his debut essay collection, award-winning poet Jaswinder Bolina meditates on "how race," as he puts it, "becomes metaphysical": the cumulative toll of the microaggressions and macro-pressures lurking in the academic market, on the literary circuit, and on the sidewalks of any given U.S. city. Training a thoughtful lens on questions about immigration and assimilation and class, *Of Color* is a bold, expansive, and finally optimistic diagnosis of present-day America.

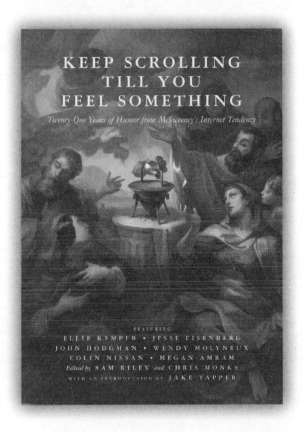

"I couldn't put down Keep Scrolling Till You Feel Something
but then the sheer weight of this massive book ripped off both of my arms."
—Chad Nackers, Editor-in-Chief of The Onion

KEEP SCROLLING TILL
YOU FEEL SOMETHING
edited by Sam Riley and Chris Monks

It's a great undertaking to raise a humor website from infancy to full-fledged adulthood, but with the right editors, impeccable taste, and a dire political landscape, your site will enjoy years of relevance and comic validation. Featuring brand-new pieces and classics by some of today's best humor writers, like Ellie Kemper, Wendy Molyneux, Jesse Eisenberg, Tim Carvell, Karen Chee, Colin Nissan, Megan Amram, and many more.

ALSO AVAILABLE
FROM McSWEENEY'S

POETRY

COLLINS LIBRARY

ALL THIS AND MORE AT

STORE.MCSWEENEYS.NET

Founded in 1998, McSweeney's is an independent publisher based in San Francisco. McSweeney's exists to champion ambitious and inspired new writing, and to challenge conventional expectations about where it's found, how it looks, and who participates. We're here to discover things we love, help them find their most resplendent form, and place them into the hands of curious, engaged readers.

THERE ARE SEVERAL WAYS TO SUPPORT MCSWEENEY'S:

Support Us on Patreon
visit *www.patreon.com/mcsweeneysinternettendency*

Subscribe & Shop
visit *store.mcsweeneys.net*

Volunteer & Intern
email *eric@mcsweeneys.net*

Sponsor Books & *Quarterlies*
email *amanda@mcsweeneys.net*

To learn more, please visit *www.mcsweeneys.net/donate*
or contact Executive Director Amanda Uhle at
amanda@mcsweeneys.net or 415.642.5609.

McSweeney's Literary Arts Fund is a nonprofit
organization as described by IRS 501(c)(3).
Your support is invaluable to us.